1850

AS History
UNIT 1

Edexcel

The Seeds of Evil: The Rise of
National Socialism in Germany to 1933

Geoff Stewart

Series E...phy

Philip Allan Updates
Market Place
Deddington
Oxfordshire
OX15 0SE

tel: 01869 338652
fax: 01869 337590
e-mail: sales@philipallan.co.uk
www.philipallan.co.uk

© Philip Allan Updates 2001
Reprinted October 2003

ISBN-13 978-0-860034-94-0
ISBN-10 0-860034-94-1

This Guide has been written specifically to support students preparing for the Edexcel AS History Unit 1 examination. The content has been neither approved nor endorsed by Edexcel and remains the sole responsibility of the author.

Typeset by Alden Bookset, Oxford
Printed by Information Press, Eynsham, Oxford

Contents

Introduction

■ ■ ■

Content Guidance

■ ■ ■

Questions and Answers

Introduction

Aims of the unit

Unit 1 amounts to 20% of the whole A-level course or 40% of the AS award. It requires knowledge of the topic and the ability to assess and use the source material provided. The source-handling skills expected are similar to those required at GCSE but more developed. The difficulty of the source material and questions asked is less than for the full A-level set in Unit 6.

The total of marks for Unit 1 is 60. These are split roughly into 20 marks for knowledge of the topic and 40 marks for the ability to handle the sources.

Handling the sources involves:
- interpreting, evaluating and using a range of source material
- explaining and evaluating interpretations of the historical events and topics studied

Knowledge involves:
- recalling, selecting and deploying historical knowledge accurately
- communicating knowledge and understanding of history in a clear and effective manner
- presenting historical explanations to show an understanding of appropriate concepts
- arriving at substantiated judgements

The emphasis of this unit is on the comprehension and manipulation of the source extracts rather than on a simple knowledge of the rise of the Nazis. As you will see in the Question and Answer section, only one question, (b), is a test of basic knowledge, and is usually worth 10 marks. Questions (a), (c) and (d) are all tests of skill in comprehension and assessment of the sources, and require no information other than that provided in the extracts. The last question, (e), carries the highest number of marks (24 out of 60). This question, as might be expected, is the most demanding as it requires both knowledge and the ability to manipulate the appropriate extracts. A good answer will keep a sharp focus on the question asked, combining both knowledge and the source materials provided.

It is extremely important to take note of the number of marks allocated to each section and to make sure that your effort is appropriate to the spread of marks. In other words, the response to question (e) should be roughly four times as long as the response to question (a).

When the word '**study**' is used at the beginning of a question it is an indication that no additional knowledge is required (although clearly such knowledge might help you to comprehend or evaluate the source). Where it is necessary to use your own knowledge, this will be stated clearly in the question.

The examination paper

On the examination paper for this unit you will be given sources that add up to no more than 500 words. One of the sources, usually the last, will be a secondary source. One of the sources will usually be visual or statistical. Before each source you will be given some information in italics. This is intended to help you understand the nature of the source and is particularly important when it comes to dealing with the visual source.

Five sample questions are given in the last section of this book. Study them carefully. In each case the sources are followed by a question in five parts.

- Part (a) is normally a test of your comprehension of, or ability to make inferences from, a primary source. It usually carries only 3 or 4 marks and therefore does not warrant a lengthy answer.
- Part (b) is a stimulus question. You will need to draw upon your own knowledge to explain either the meaning of an important concept or the role and/or importance of a key individual, group or institution. You will not be able to answer the question by simply copying out large sections from the source. That would be a waste of time.
- Part (c) is usually a cross-referencing question. This means comparing the content of a couple of sources and reaching a conclusion based on the comparison. Typically, this would involve asking how far one source could be used to support or contradict another source.
- Part (d) usually requires you to appraise or evaluate sources. You will be asked to evaluate the usefulness or reliability of one or two pieces of primary source material in relation to a specific purpose or inquiry. This last point is very important. You will not be asked about the general usefulness of the particular sources. You will always be directed to a particular and specific inquiry.
- Part (e) is the most important. It is a lead-out question, in which you will have to blend your knowledge and one or two of the sources in a focused answer to an essay question. A typical question will start with **explain how** or **explain why**.

The layout of the questions on the examination paper is as follows:

(a) Study Source 4
  What, according to this source, were the reasons for X?   (6 marks)

(b) Use your own knowledge to explain what Y was.   (10 marks)

(c) Study Sources 3 and 4
  **What evidence in Source 3 supports the views expressed in Source 4 about
  the nature of X?**   (10 marks)

(d) Study Sources 1 and 2
  How useful are these two sources to a historian studying Z?   (10 marks)

(e) Study Sources 2 and 4 and use your own knowledge
  Explain how important X was to Y.   (24 marks)

How to use this guide

Although the emphasis of this unit is on the handling of sources, you still need to learn the facts. Carefully study the outline material in the Content Guidance section. Try to:

- master the vocabulary and the concepts given there
- sort out clearly in your mind the important individuals who figure in the events of the period in question
- remember the people in terms of the parties and groupings to which they belonged

The most important part of the guide is the Question and Answer section, which provides five examples of the sort of questions you will be asked. It is important to work through each of these, studying the two sample answers provided and the examiner's comments (preceded by the icon *e*). The first example is an A-grade response which, although not perfect, gives a good idea of what is required. The purpose of the second answer is to illustrate some of the common errors that students make.

The sources

There is a vast range of sources available to students studying the rise of the Nazi Party. New books appear almost daily on the subject. There are many collections of primary documents relevant to this topic and students should familiarise themselves with some of the different types of material available. The Question and Answer section of this guide contains an assortment of these. As with all sources of evidence used by historians, it is important to try to find out when and why a particular document was written. Usually the date will be given in italics before the extract, and some information will be provided to help you understand why this particular source was originally produced. Clearly it helps to know the political sympathies of the author. Was the author or illustrator a Nazi sympathiser or supporter? Was he or she an opponent of the Nazis, such as John Heartfield, an artist used in one of the documents in the Question and Answer section? Bias is inevitable, but this does not mean that the sources are worthless to historians.

It is, of course, important to realise that people's opinions change over time and with circumstances. Hitler and the Nazi Party were no exception. Two of the most important sources of information used by historians in their study of the origins and development of the Nazi Party are:

- *Mein Kampf* ('My Struggle'), written by Hitler in 1924 and regularly used by historians to illustrate Hitler's opinions on a variety of subjects
- the so-called 25 *Points*, the Nazi Party programme written in 1920

Extracts from both these works are given in the Question and Answer section. How important these two documents are is open to debate. Some have argued that Hitler was later ashamed and embarrassed by much of what he had written in 1924. Doubt has also been cast on the value of the 25 *Points*, written as they were in the very early days of the party. The Nazi Party of 1920 was very different from the mass party of 1933. The party was particularly adept at adjusting to circumstances, targeting the working class in the mid-1920s but switching very effectively to win over the peasantry from 1928. In the early 1930s it was very successful in gaining the support of large sections of the middle classes. Clearly its propaganda varied according to the circumstances. The examples given in the Question and Answer section are intended to illustrate both the flexibility and the considerable ambiguity that was present in the Nazi Party. In some ways the party was all things to all people because it lacked a clear-cut message. It was both socialist and nationalist, as its very name implies. Traditionally Hitler is considered a figure of the right, particularly by Marxists and those of left-wing persuasion. Yet to many contemporary conservatives he was a dangerous figure of the left, closely related to the communists he denounced. Many of the Nazis' most bitter opponents came from the ranks of the aristocracy and the traditional right.

'Who supported the Nazi Party, and why?' are two of the big questions within this topic that historians have tried to answer for decades. Many of the extracts used in the Question and Answer section are concerned with these two questions. The dates of such extracts must always be taken into account. This is particularly important when dealing with the rise of the Nazi Party, in view of its very rapid transformation between 1929 and 1933. Try to pay attention to the social class of the writer as this may be vital. However, just because one Hamburg schoolteacher supported (or opposed) the Nazi Party does not mean that all schoolteachers or all people in Hamburg were Nazi supporters or opponents. This also introduces the importance of geography. Nazi support varied from one part of Germany to another.

Don't forget that opponents can become supporters and supporters opponents. General Erich von Ludendorff worked closely with Hitler during the Munich Putsch but 10 years later, when Hitler became Chancellor, Ludendorff famously denounced him as 'accursed' and 'a man who would lead Germany into the abyss'.

The visual and statistical sources may pose particular problems to some candidates. With cartoons it is especially important to read and understand the accompanying information to enable you to make sense of them. A cartoon represents the opinion of one person — either that of the artist or the proprietor of the journal in which it appears — possibly both. It is likely, however, that it will also appeal to a wider audience, who will buy the journal in the expectation of certain opinions.

Statistical data have their own special pitfalls. Always look carefully to see what is being offered. Once again, dates are important. When election results are provided, make sure you understand what is referred to — number of MPs elected or percentage of the vote cast for a particular party. Look carefully at the relative performance of different parties. Finally, do not be intimidated by the appearance of statistical data. Some people are frightened by statistics, but they are a very useful way of presenting a complex mass of information simply.

Examinable skills

The ability to comprehend a source is perhaps the most basic one required in this unit. To achieve this there is no substitute for simple practice. Analysis, evaluation and interpretation follow on from the basic capacity for comprehension.

When answering the comprehension question do not write out the source in the hope that this will provide the examiner with the answer. It is essential to select the appropriate material to answer the question set. The answer should be as brief and concise as possible.

The stimulus question requires precisely selected 'own knowledge'.

When it comes to tackling the cross-referencing question, which involves the comprehension of two sources, it is important to avoid simply paraphrasing the sources. The question requires you to offer explanations based on the two extracts. Your answer should have a clear direction and should address the question throughout — not just at the end. Where necessary you should make appropriate inferences and deductions from the source extracts. Begin with a clear opening statement that shows where your answer is going. Develop your points in a logical and structured way with appropriate quotations and support from the extracts. These should not be too long. You should be using the extracts, not allowing yourself to be dictated to by them.

The source evaluation question often invites a pre-prepared answer about bias and the nature of primary and secondary sources. It must be emphasised that your evaluation of the source is for a specific purpose. You must shape your answer by constantly showing awareness of the question asked. Points need to be supported by specific reference to the extracts where appropriate — though quotations should not be lengthy.

The final essay answer involves the most skills. Focus on the question asked. It is essential that you use both your own knowledge and appropriate evidence from the sources. One of the skills looked for is the ability to **communicate clear, concise and logical arguments substantiated by relevant evidence**. The ability to write clearly and well is one of the most valuable in the historian's armoury. It is a skill to be worked on constantly. There is no quick fix to achieve literary polish. However, candidates must remember that there should be a clear introductory statement and, most important of all, a conclusion to draw together the argument advanced throughout the answer.

Content
Guidance

The areas covered by Unit 1 are:
- the Nazi Party from its formation to the Beer Hall Putsch
- Nazi beliefs about, and policies towards, Weimar politics and society
- economic, social and political reasons for the support of, and opposition to, the Nazis to 1933
- Hitler and German politics, 1929–33

The main focus is on the growth and development of the Nazi Party between 1920 and March 1933. A knowledge and understanding of Weimar politics is essential to this. You will need to understand why Hitler and the Nazis so detested the young republic. Though no questions on foreign policy will be set, a knowledge of the Treaty of Versailles and an understanding of the hostility it evoked are vital to understanding the success of the Nazis.

To help you appreciate what you will need to learn, the subject matter of Unit 1 has been broken down in the Content Guidance section in two ways. First, there is an outline of topics — for use as a checklist for revision before the exam. Second, there is an introduction to the basic information, concepts and personalities you will need to know about. These are covered in five areas:

(1) Germany and Hitler to 1920 (pages 13–18)

(2) The social, economic and political background to the rise of the Nazis (pages 18–22)

(3) The quiet years, 1925–28 (pages 22–26)

(4) The Nazi breakthrough to power, 1929–33 (pages 26–33)

(5) The consolidation of power, January–March 1933 (pages 33–36)

Each of these is followed by listings of concepts and key figures. Words which appear in these listings are emboldened in the text.

Outline of topics

Background to 1920

Germany in 1914 — the Second Reich
The experience of the First World War, 1914–18
The revolution of 1918
The Treaty of Versailles, 1919
The Weimar Constitution
Weimar political parties and politics

The economic, social and political context, 1920–33

The crisis years, 1920–23
The golden years, 1924–28
The economic crisis, 1929 — agriculture, industry and trade
The onset of the political crisis, 1929–30
The political crisis, 1930–33

Hitler and the early years of the Nazi Party to 1924

Hitler 1889–1920
Hitler's ideas and the formation and growth of the Nazi Party in Munich,
  1920–22
The Munich Beer Hall Putsch, 1923
Landsberg and *Mein Kampf*, 1924

The re-establishment of the party and its organisation, 1925–28

Hitler reasserts control — Bamberg
The social profile of party membership — who was a Nazi and why
Party structure and planning
The 1928 election and the situation in rural areas

The breakthrough to national importance, 1928–30

The appeal of the National Socialist German Workers' Party (NSDAP)
  to the peasants
The appeal to youth
Hitler, Hugenberg and the Young Plan
Goebbels and the election of 1930

The struggle for power, September 1930–January 1933

The role of the SA — Stennes' Revolt
The drift of the middle classes to the NSDAP — the communist menace
Hitler's balancing act — the Harzburg Front and relations with the
  German National People's Party (DNVP)
The presidential elections, 1932

The July election, 1932
The November election, 1932
The attitude of the elite and the army
The coming to power, January 1933

The creation of a Nazi dictatorship, January–March 1933

The position of Hitler and the Nazis in the Cabinet — the extent of their power
Negotiations with the army and big business in February
The Reichstag fire and the Emergency Decrees
The March elections
The Enabling Bill

Germany and Hitler to 1920

Germany 1914–20

Germany in 1914 was the greatest power in Europe. It had the world's most powerful army and the world's second most powerful navy. In every way Germany appeared to be one of the world's leading nations. German industry was second only to that of the USA in volume of production. Since the beginning of the 1900s Germany had overtaken Britain as an industrial power. It was in the new industries of the twentieth century that Germany particularly shone. In chemicals, engineering and the new electrical industries Britain was left far behind. As the German economy expanded, wages and living standards rose. In the1880s Germany developed a national welfare system in advance of any other country, with old age pensions and health insurance. But Germans did not live by bread alone. In the realm of ideas and culture Germany was pre-eminent. The greatest names in philosophy and music were German. Not surprisingly most Germans, whatever their political persuasion, felt rightly proud of the achievements of their new nation. None felt this more than their ruler, **Kaiser Wilhelm II**.

This new Germany was created in 1871, when the German state of Prussia conquered France and joined with the other German states in a new German empire — the **Second Reich**. The King of Prussia had become the German Emperor, head of an imperial federation of smaller German states like Baden and Bavaria. This new Germany was no democracy — despite the existence of a parliament (the Reichstag). The Kaiser appointed the chancellor (prime minister) and the Kaiser was the only person who could remove him. The Kaiser was also head of the army, which enjoyed enormous prestige. A landowning gentry and aristocracy dominated the army and political life. The new industrial élite shared power with them, but very much as junior partners.

The largest party in the Reichstag in 1914 was the Social Democratic Party of Germany (SPD), which claimed to speak for the new and growing working class. There was considerable tension between the socialists, who wanted to abolish the monarchy and turn Germany into a real democracy, and the old élite who, not surprisingly, felt somewhat threatened by this large party that spoke the language of revolution and **Marxism**. In reality the SPD was no longer a revolutionary party — but it wanted real political changes and it frightened the Kaiser and the army.

The outbreak of war in 1914 seemed at first to help solve some of these internal problems. Even the SPD rallied to the war effort, believing that the war was a just one forced on Germany by an envious coalition of France, Russia and Britain. This spirit of unity and national pride was something the Nazis were to seek to recapture after the war. As the war continued — with mounting casualties at the front and growing hunger and suffering at home — so this spirit of unity began to unravel. The British naval blockade of Germany, by cutting off food supplies, caused immense suffering.

It has been estimated that half a million Germans died of malnutrition. By 1917, with the war in its third year and stalemate on the Western Front with France, the cries for peace increased, as did the number of strikes in Germany. The collapse of Russia in 1917 offered one last hope of victory despite the USA's declaration of war in April 1917. However, if Germany failed to act quickly it would be overwhelmed by the USA's economic might.

By late 1917, critical decisions were being made by the army. Germany had turned into a virtual military dictatorship under **Field Marshal Paul von Hindenburg** and his deputy, **General Erich von Ludendorff**. Hindenburg and Ludendorff decided to gamble everything on one last great push for victory in March 1918. It nearly succeeded. The German armies came closer to Paris than at any time since 1914. It cost 800,000 casualties, however — losses the Germans could not afford. A devastating Allied counterattack followed, beginning in July.

Germany's failure to achieve victory saw morale in the army plummet. At home, strikes multiplied. The war was lost and even the army High Command recognised this — although later they were to deny it. Ludendorff recommended that the Kaiser appoint a new liberal government to seek peace.

Many Germans still believed that a generous peace would be offered by the Allies — in line with the '14 Points' laid down by US President Wilson in January 1918. But this expectation was unreal. Germany was in a far weaker position by October. Great suffering had been inflicted on France and Allied troops in the meantime. Germany had imposed a brutally harsh treaty on Russia in March 1918. The Allies offered an armistice, to take effect on 11 November 1918. Details of a permanent peace would be given later. The Germans agreed, signing up to the armistice in a railway carriage in a clearing in the forest of Compiègne.

The events of the autumn of 1918 were later to be shrouded in myth and lies. Many Germans convinced themselves that they had been tricked by the Allies: that they could have fought on and would certainly have done so had they known of the harshness of the treaty that was to be offered them in 1919. There was a widespread belief, held by many in the army, that Germany had been stabbed in the back by revolutionaries and strikers. Jews were said to have played a major part in this, a view held by Hitler and, incidentally, by the Kaiser himself. It was convenient for many — not least those in the military who had lost their nerve in 1918 — to blame defeat on a nebulous conspiracy of 'reds', foreigners and politicians — those later described by Hitler as the **November Criminals**.

Revolution accompanied the armistice in Germany. The Kaiser fled to Holland and a republic was proclaimed. In the minds of many, the republic was associated with national humiliation and the end of the monarchy. This humiliation became more pronounced when the terms of the peace treaty were made clear to the Germans in 1919. The loss of Alsace and Lorraine to France could be accepted; the loss of so much territory to Poland could not. Over 1 million Germans found themselves citizens of the new Polish state. The Allies had claimed that the treaty was based on the principle of self-determination, yet millions of Austrian Germans were forbidden to join the Reich. Germany's colonies were taken away and distributed among the victorious Allies. Most Germans convinced themselves that the whole treaty was grossly unfair.

The enforced disarmament of Germany was bitterly resented. Its magnificent army was reduced to 100,000 men, smaller than the army of the new and despised state of Poland. Its new navy was destroyed and Germany was forbidden to build a replacement. Germany was to have no air force and the army was to have no tanks. The left bank of the Rhine was to be permanently demilitarised and Allied troops were to maintain garrisons on the right bank for 15 years. Most resented of all was the so-called 'war guilt' clause. Germany was declared to be responsible for the First World War — and faced a huge bill for its cost, imposed by the Allies. These reparations, more than anything else, were to make the ***diktat*** of the Treaty of Versailles a source of anger for many Germans.

In January 1919 a group of extremist socialists tried to seize power in a confusing revolution. It was crushed by the ***Freikorps*** and the moderate socialist government of **Friedrich Ebert**. A similar 'red' rising took place in Munich in the spring and was crushed by the army. Meanwhile, a battered and starving Germany was given a new constitution. To avoid the revolution in Berlin, delegates met in the nearby town of Weimar — hence the new regime was called the Weimar Republic. It was carefully constructed to try to provide Germany with its first real taste of democracy. The head of state, the president, was to be elected every 7 years. The president appointed the chancellor, who would head the government of the Reich. It was assumed that the chancellor would enjoy the support of the majority of the political parties in the German parliament, or Reichstag. There were to be elections every 4 years using a simple system of proportional representation. Electors voted for a party and each party produced a list of candidates numbered in order of importance within the party. The result of this system was that each party won a proportion of parliamentary seats directly related to its share of the votes cast. However, the system tended to prevent any one party having an effective majority. It encouraged the formation of a large number of **political parties** representing many different shades of political opinion — **monarchists**, conservatives, liberals and socialists. It ensured that every government was a coalition. During the Weimar years strong and effective decision-making was difficult and governments came and went with regularity.

Hitler and the forerunners of the NSDAP

In many ways Hitler was a very ordinary man made extraordinary by circumstance. He was born in 1889 into a lower-middle-class family on the Austrian side of the German–Austrian border. From his home town he made his way to Vienna in 1907. This was then a German city, but as the capital of a vast and largely Slav empire it contained many races, including a large Jewish minority. **Anti-Semitism** was rife and was already part of the currency of city politics. The then Mayor of Vienna, Carl Lüger, was a noted anti-Semite.

Hitler was heavily influenced by the ideas and emotions in the operas of **Richard Wagner**, spending much of his small private allowance on tickets for these grand events. He loved the magical world, where good and evil wrestled in an eternal struggle. He also absorbed the rabid German nationalism preached by street-corner orators and present in many cheap pamphlets. He increasingly saw life as a struggle between Jewish demons and German superheroes. Hitler absorbed the twin bedrock ideas of his life — racialism and nationalism — before the First World War. However, it was the events of 1918–19 that translated his prejudices into passions. Hitler blamed Germany's defeat in 1918 on the Jews. He returned to Munich in 1919, only to have his growing anti-Semitism confirmed by the prominent role Jews played in the abortive revolution there. Hitler increasingly believed that there existed a vast, all-embracing Jewish conspiracy to destroy civilisation. Were not Jews dominant among the Bolsheviks in Russia? Had not Jewish capital in America, Britain and France mobilised those countries for the defeat of Germany? Passion and hatred gave power to his voice. Simple, easily understood prejudices poured out to the first political audiences to hear him in Munich in 1920. The simplicity of his message ensured a favourable reception in a city looking for scapegoats — tired and exhausted by war and revolution.

In some ways what Hitler was offering was a new political religion shaped for the age of the common individual. Even before the First World War all those devices that would have kept Hitler firmly in check were weakening. The German philosopher Nietzsche had famously declared God to be dead. Traditional religion and churches were losing their grip. The old ruling élites were being challenged. An age of mass consumption and mass ideas was being born. Kings and emperors were replaced by politicians telling the people what they wanted to hear in language they could readily grasp. The First World War speeded the destruction of the old world, particularly in Germany. With the Kaiser gone, a new icon was needed. The returning disillusioned troops were particularly vulnerable to the sort of simplistic message that Hitler propounded. The war had brutalised many and made violence respectable. The new National Socialist German Workers' Party (NSDAP), founded in 1920, was to provide a home for soldiers like Ernst Röhm, who flaunted his contempt for conventional morality. The displaced Baltic German Alfred Rosenberg, fleeing from the Bolsheviks, also joined the new party, echoing Hitler's bitter anti-Jewish sentiments and racial analysis of the world.

Glossary and concepts

anti-Semitism — hostility towards Jews. There was widespread anti-Jewish feeling in France and Russia in the 1890s. From Russia came one of the most famous pieces of anti-Jewish propaganda, the Protocols of the Elders of Zion. This claimed to show a worldwide Jewish conspiracy and it certainly influenced many Nazi writers and thinkers.

diktat — word used to describe the Treaty of Versailles, meaning 'dictate'. The German delegates at the peace conference were not given the option to negotiate but were presented with a document that they had to sign, or else face renewal of the war.

Freikorps — paramilitary organisations established after the end of the First World War. Members were often drawn from ex-officers of the German army. They were active on the eastern border of Germany, defending Germans in the chaos which followed the border changes of the Versailles Treaty. They also played a major part in attacking left-wing revolutionaries in German cities.

Marxism — a set of political beliefs based on the works of Karl Marx. Marx claimed to have invented scientific socialism, showing the inevitable triumph of the working class or proletariat over the bourgeoisie. The Social Democratic Party of Germany (SPD) claimed to be Marxist but by 1914 had lost much of its revolutionary fervour. The Bolshevik revolution in Russia brought revolutionary Marxists to power there and they claimed that they would spread Marxism throughout Europe. Marxists believed in the common ownership of the means of production, distribution and exchange, i.e. they wanted the state to take over most forms of property. This created fear among those with property.

monarchists — people in Weimar Germany who supported the return of the monarchy and the abolition of the republic. The DNVP was a monarchist party opposed to the revolution of 1918.

November Criminals — those blamed by Hitler for the loss of the war and for the Treaty of Versailles. These included many of the leading politicians of the Weimar Republic.

political parties — Weimar Germany had a number of significant political parties. The DNVP (German National People's Party) was a conservative party drawing its support from rich landowners and big business. It was opposed to the Weimar Republic and was anxious to see the return of the monarchy. The DVP (German People's Party) was a moderate conservative party drawing support from the middle classes and business community. It was prepared to work with other parties to produce coalition democratic government. Its leading member was Gustav Stresemann, who became Chancellor in 1923 and then served as Foreign Minister until his death in 1929. The DDP (Germany Democratic Party) was a liberal party which supported the Weimar Republic. It enjoyed support from the lower middle classes and small farmers. The Centre Party was a religious or confessional party which spoke for Catholics and the Catholic Church. It drew support from south and western Germany. Unlike the other parties, it crossed class boundaries in its support. The SPD was the largest party of the Weimar Republic and its most consistent supporter. It was nominally Marxist but in reality it was a moderate reformist party, drawing its support from the skilled working class in the urban areas of Germany. The KPD, the Communist Party of Germany, was thoroughly Marxist and closely connected to the new Bolshevik government in Moscow (from which it received support). It normally gained around 10% of the vote, usually from the younger workers in the big cities like Hamburg and Berlin.

Second Reich — name given to the period of German history between 1871 and 1918. The First Reich had ended in 1806 and had dated back to its founder, Charlemagne.

Key figures

Friedrich Ebert (1871–1925) — a moderate socialist and a leader of the SPD who became the first president of the Weimar Republic. His cooperation with the army in 1919 was vital in crushing the extreme left wing and preventing a Russian-style revolution.

Field Marshal Paul von Hindenburg (1847–1934) — professional soldier drawn from an aristocratic East German background who became a national hero in 1914 when he defeated two Russian armies. He became Commander-in-Chief in 1916 and remained the nominal head of Germany's fighting forces until 1918. In 1925 he was persuaded by the political parties of the right to stand as President. He won and brought stability to the Weimar Republic. He remained President until his death in 1934.

General Erich von Ludendorff (1865–1937) — professional German soldier and usually held to be the brains behind the partnership he shared with Hindenburg during the First World War. After the war he became associated with various right-wing causes and drifted into alliance with Hitler in 1923. He escaped prosecution for the Munich Putsch and became increasingly suspicious of Hitler, whom he criticised.

Richard Wagner (1813–83) — German composer who had enormous influence upon Hitler. The romantic operas known as the Ring Cycle composed between 1853 and 1874 particularly moved the young Hitler, who was later to claim that a knowledge of Wagner was essential to understand National Socialism.

Kaiser Wilhelm II (1859–1941) — third and last emperor of modern Germany. He abdicated in November 1918 and spent the rest of his life in Holland as an exile. Like Hitler, he blamed the Jews for the Germans having lost the First World War.

The social, economic and political background to the rise of the Nazis

The Weimar Republic

The first 4 years of the Weimar Republic, between 1919 and 1923, might easily have been the last. The republic was beset by problems, so much so that a foreign observer could have been forgiven for thinking the whole democratic experiment a disaster. A lot of Germans certainly did. These years witnessed the slide into **hyperinflation**. Many middle-class Germans were ruined. Those living on fixed pensions or relying on cash savings saw their value dwindle to nothing. Those who had patriotically bought government bonds during the war now found them worthless. In January 1920 the exchange rate had fallen to 65 marks to US$1. By 15 November 1923, US$1 was worth 42,000,000,000,000 marks.

Germany's effective bankruptcy brought one benefit for the government — though at a terrible price for the German people. The falling value of the mark eroded the vast and unsustainable mountain of debt that the First World War had bequeathed to the nation. However, economic chaos left the middle class disillusioned from the first with the new democratic Germany, distancing the republic from a natural constituency of support. The introduction of a new currency on 15 November 1923 was eventually to bring stability but it did not restore prosperity to those who had been ruined.

Politically, the years 1919–23 were marked by many of the signs of a society in disintegration. Political assassination became commonplace, the victims being for the most part supporters of democracy and the perpetrators being drawn from the radical right who hated the new republic. Most army officers disliked the democratic republic and clung to the traditions of the empire. Judges, senior civil servants and university professors longed, for the most part, for the return of the monarchy. The judges showed their bias in the way they treated the perpetrators of political assassination. Murders of figures on the right were more likely to carry the death penalty than murders of figures on the left.

The new republic was threatened with revolt from both left and right. In 1920 a group of ex-army officers under General von Luttwitz and a senior civil servant, Dr Kapp, tried to seize power by force. They were defeated by a general strike. In the same week as these events were taking place in Berlin, a communist group of workers tried to seize power in the Ruhr, the industrial heartland of Germany. This uprising was crushed by the army. A year later there were fresh communist disturbances in Hamburg and central Germany. Many property owners were terrified that Germany would go the same way as Russia, where the new Bolshevik government was consolidating its power.

Bedevilling the government was the need to meet Allied demands for reparations. This added to the weakness of the currency. The nation's gold and foreign currency reserves were exhausted. In desperation, Germany resorted to trying to pay in kind with, for example, telegraph poles and coal, but the British already had too much of the latter and the French demand for the former was strictly limited. In 1922 Germany declared that it could no longer pay.

The French retaliated by occupying the Ruhr. German workers went on strike in protest and were supported by the Weimar government, which met the bill by printing money. Germany's currency went into free-fall throughout 1923. Foreign visitors could live like kings on their dollars and pounds, much to the resentment of native Germans. Unsurprisingly, 1923 brought fresh outbreaks of violence from both right and left. In the autumn there were communist risings in Saxony that later spread to Hamburg and Thuringia. In Munich, Hitler felt his time had come. His abortive attempt at a coup — the Munich Beer Hall **Putsch** — was launched in November. The Reichstag elections showed gains for the Communist Party and the extreme right. Democracy seemed — and was — far from secure.

The NSDAP from 1920 to December 1924

In January 1919 Anton Drexler, a locksmith, founded a small and insignificant political party called the German Workers' Party, or DAP. It met in a pub and the party funds were kept in a cigar box. Drexler and his few comrades seemed to feel that the parties of the left lacked patriotism and that the parties of the right lacked social conscience. His party, he hoped, would combine the two.

Hitler returned to Munich in 1919 and witnessed the traumatic events of the attempt to seize power by German Bolsheviks. He remained with the army, serving as a political intelligence officer. The army was intent on keeping an eye on potential troublemakers. Drexler's party was seen as a potential source of trouble and Hitler was sent to observe their meetings. He appears to have been so impressed by the party's ideas that he joined in September. He continued in the army until March 1920.

The party he joined was one of many similar *völkisch* groups that existed in Germany. There were 15 alone in Munich, symptomatic of the discontent of postwar Germany. All shared a hatred of the Treaty of Versailles and a sense of betrayal by the politicians of the republic. Most were bitterly anti-Semitic. While still officially a member of the army, Hitler, with Drexler, drew up the DAP's political programme, known as the *25 Points*. It was to remain unaltered although largely ignored.

Hitler was a considerable catch for the small party. He quickly showed a talent for public speaking far beyond that of any other member. He became its biggest attraction, capable of bringing crowds to meetings and thus covering the party's expenses. DAP membership grew. In January 1920 there had been only 190 party members. By the end of the year this had grown to 2,000. In December 1920 the party was able to fund its own newspaper, the *Völkischer Beobachter*.

For Hitler's political career, 1921 was to prove a vital year. A major dispute developed within the ranks of the newly renamed National Socialist German Workers' Party (NSDAP or Nazi Party). Some members wanted to merge with another rival right-wing fringe party. Hitler objected. Compromise and negotiation were not his way. It was all or nothing. When he appeared to be losing the argument he resigned from the party. It was a tremendous gamble but it paid off. The fledgling NSDAP could not afford to lose its best speaker. Hitler was welcomed back in triumph in July, made leader and granted dictatorial powers within the party. Increasingly he referred to himself as the drummer, the man who would mobilise the masses for Germany's regeneration. He still does not appear to have thought of himself as the would-be dictator of Germany — merely as the person who would make Germany's regeneration possible.

The other major development of 1921 was the formation of the *Sturmabteilung* (SA) (literally the 'Storm Section' but often referred to as the brownshirts). The SA's origins went back to 1920 when the party needed bouncers to protect its political meetings. A group was formed to provide this service — becoming known as the gym and sports section of the party. In July 1921 this section was renamed the SA. The key figure in the SA's development was **Ernst Röhm**, a brutal former front-line captain who enjoyed violence. He filled the SA with similar-minded ex-soldiers who liked nothing better than a punch-up with rival political groups. The knuckle-duster and the cosh were important ingredients in the early days of the rise of the Nazis. Another significant figure in the early SA was Lieutenant Klintsch. Klintsch was suspected of being involved in the assassination of the Reich Foreign Minister in 1922. Within the SA he spent much of his time ensuring that the same didn't happen to Hitler, whose bodyguard he became.

By the beginning of 1922 NSDAP membership reached 6,000 but it was still largely confined to Munich. However, during 1922 the party expanded into the north of Bavaria, achieving a real base in the Protestant part of the state, especially around the ancient city of Nuremberg. The secret of this success lay in the willingness of the NSDAP to clash violently with their political opponents. This they did in a major demonstration in the town of Coburg, fighting a pitched battle with supporters of the SPD. Also in 1922, the NSDAP enjoyed an enormous stroke of luck when the leader of a rival right-wing group in Nuremberg, Julius Streicher, offered his and his party's allegiance to Hitler. The following year Streicher established another Nazi newspaper, *Der Stürmer*, which offered a diet of popular anti-Semitism heavily spiced with sex and violence.

The year 1922 offered Hitler and the Nazis another influential model of political action. In Italy, Mussolini had come to power as Prime Minister after what was, effectively, a political coup known as 'the march on Rome'. For propaganda purposes this was portrayed as a seizure of power and became part of fascist legend. In reality it had more in common with a publicity stunt — but Mussolini was not one to allow truth to get in the way of his own political progress. In November 1922 one of Hitler's sidekicks in the party proclaimed in Munich, 'Germany's Mussolini is called Adolf Hitler'. The idea of seizing power through direct action clearly had an appeal within the NSDAP.

By 1923 the party had a membership of 20,000. In the course of this year of hyper-inflation and domestic crises, membership was to touch 55,000. The French occupation of the Ruhr in January 1923 triggered what seemed to be a terminal crisis for the Weimar Republic. Nationalist outrage reached a frenzied peak. An anti-republican government came to power in Bavaria. Hitler — in cooperation with the First World War Commander Ludendorff — became convinced that he and others on the right in Bavaria could lead a march on Berlin to overthrow the republican democracy there. He assumed the cooperation of the Bavarian authorities and the German army stationed in Bavaria. This was the origin of the famous Munich Beer Hall Putsch in November. Hitler badly overestimated the broader political and public support available for such a move. He failed to win over the conservative political leaders of the state of Bavaria. The following day, in desperation, he launched a street march that ended in disaster. Armed police opened fire on the marching ranks of the NSDAP. Hitler's supporter, **Hermann Goering**, received a bullet in the groin and the man marching next to Hitler was shot dead. Hitler was arrested for treason and could reasonably expect the death penalty. The NSDAP was banned.

Hitler's trial, however, turned into a political triumph. The wide coverage it received in the press made him, for the first time, a national figure in Germany. He was the hero of the fanatic right — the man who had stood up for Germany in a time of need.

The judge was sympathetic and Hitler received a sentence of 5 years' detention in the fortress-prison of Landsberg. While in prison, Hitler was treated as a celebrity. The terms of his imprisonment were not harsh. He had the best room available. He could see visitors and mix with other party members who were also in jail. And he had the time to write **Mein Kampf** ('My Struggle'), his very own political testament. After having served only a fraction of his sentence Hitler was released, just before Christmas 1924.

Glossary and concepts

hyperinflation — crisis involving the value of the currency when prices increase so rapidly that money loses almost all value. Good for debtors, bad for savers.

Mein Kampf ('My Struggle') — Hitler's autobiography and reflections on life, as well as a type of political manifesto. *Mein Kampf* was published in two volumes in 1925 and 1926.

putsch — an attempt to seize power by force.

völkisch — racial or ethnic.

Key figures

Hermann Goering (1893–1945) — joined the Nazi Party in 1922, and was a good catch for the party. His father had been governor of German southwest Africa and he himself was an officer in the German Air Force in the First World War, achieving fame as an air ace. He was badly injured in the Munich Putsch but became a Nazi MP in 1928. He was one of only two Nazis to be included in Hitler's first Cabinet in 1933. Throughout most of the 1930s he was second in importance only to Hitler in the party. On the establishment of the Third Reich he became Prime Minister of Prussia and Reich Air Minister — in charge of the *Luftwaffe*, the new German Air Force. Goering became Hitler's deputy in 1938 but lost influence during the course of the Second World War. He was tried in Nuremberg in 1945 but committed suicide before he could be executed.

Ernst Röhm (1887–1934) — served as a captain in the First World War and joined the Nazi Party shortly after Hitler. He enjoyed the excitement of violence and developed the SA in its early days. When the Munich Putsch failed he went abroad, but he was reappointed as commander of the SA in 1930, a post he held until June 1934, when he died in the Night of the Long Knives.

The quiet years, 1925–28

Political, social and economic background

Having survived the first 4 years of the 1920s it began to look, by 1925, as if the Weimar Republic might take root and provide Germany with both stable government and prosperity. A new currency was introduced at the end of 1923. In the course of

1924 the French were persuaded to withdraw from the Ruhr and a new deal was struck on reparations. Germany's relations with both France and Britain improved under the skilful guidance of **Gustav Stresemann**. In 1926 Germany entered the League of Nations. Once more Germany commanded a place as one of the great powers of Europe. More importantly, the German economy began to flourish. Exports boomed and new technology helped to produce new jobs. Investment flooded into the country from the USA. American banks lent money to the German government, to local authorities and to German companies. American companies set up in Germany and something of the prosperity of the USA in the 1920s came to the country.

The economic prosperity was in some ways matched and mirrored by political stability. In 1925 the socialist President, Friedrich Ebert, died and was replaced by the conservative Field Marshal Paul von Hindenburg. Hindenburg proved something of a substitute monarch, reassuring the middle classes and gaining the loyalty of the army who, if they did not love the republic, would at least accept it with Hindenburg at its head. The Reichstag elections of December 1924 and 1928 showed a decline in support for the more extreme parties. The NSDAP had picked up 6.6% of the vote in May 1924; this fell to 3% in December and was down to 2.6% in 1928. The Communist Party's share of the vote fell from 12.6% to 9% in December 1924, recovering slightly in 1928 to 10.6%. In 1928 the longest-serving coalition government of Germany was formed under Herman Müller of the SPD. It was to last until March 1930. The political assassinations that marked and marred the early years of the Weimar Republic declined sharply. It appeared that Germany had achieved stability. Yet Foreign Minister Stresemann believed the republic was 'dancing on a volcano' — and a close analysis of the situation could produce worrying conclusions.

The prosperity of the new industries was not matched by that of traditional heavy industry. Agriculture remained the biggest single employer in Germany (with over 30% of the workforce) and was in serious trouble as prices of agricultural products tumbled. Many employers increasingly resented the concessions granted to workers in the early days of the Weimar Republic. They thought the power of trade unions had grown too much and sought to claw back what they felt they had lost in 1919 and 1920. Even the prosperity of new industries was fragile, resting upon foreign export markets and constant new supplies of capital from the USA. If the capital should dry up or the export markets become saturated, then disaster could ensue.

Although the Weimar Republic had fewer political problems between 1925 and 1928, there was still cause for concern. Governments came and went with surprising rapidity, even if some ministerial posts remained in experienced hands (the position of foreign secretary was occupied by Stresemann for 5 years). There was a failure to take tough decisions. Taxation was unpopular and government spending popular. Balancing these two political truths is one of the eternal conundrums of government. Weimar Germany had first tried to solve it by printing money — with disastrous consequences in 1923. By 1925 this was no longer an option. The solution was to borrow. The federal government in Berlin, and state and even city authorities, borrowed heavily to provide a range of popular services and benefits. The policy worked well while capital was readily available. However, much of the borrowing was irresponsible.

Authorities took out short-term loans to pay for long-term projects, repaying debts as they fell due with fresh loans. Political parties still remained largely class-based or — in the case of the Centre Party — rooted in one religious community. The system of proportional representation, with its use of the list system, gave power to the party bosses in Berlin and the regional capitals. They determined the order of the candidates on the list. The link with local communities was fragile and voters became disillusioned with party politics. An ageing group of party political supremos made deals behind closed doors. The system could be tolerated as long as there was prosperity but would find it hard to deal with a real crisis.

Hitler and the NSDAP: consolidation and survival

On Hitler's release from Landsberg prison at the end of 1924, his priority was to get the ban lifted on his party. This he rapidly succeeded in doing after backstairs negotiations with senior politicians in Bavaria. He began to show real political skill, distancing himself from General Ludendorff, who was increasingly unpopular in Catholic Bavaria. He promised that the Nazi Party would not attempt any further putsch but would seek power through the ballot box.

By 1925 Hitler had reached two important conclusions with enormous consequences. First, he resolved never again to challenge the armed forces of the state but to play the Weimar Republic at its own democratic game. Second, he began to think of himself not merely as the drummer, gaining support for some other saviour of the nation, but as the chosen one, the man selected by providence to rescue Germany from humiliation and division.

Although the ban on the NSDAP was lifted, a ban was imposed on Hitler's speaking in public in most German states. He was allowed a platform only at private party meetings. The politicians of Weimar Germany calculated that this deprived the NSDAP of its chief weapon. Perhaps they were right. However, Hitler had other tasks he needed to turn to. He had to reassert his personal control over the Nazi movement and he had to pay some attention to party organisation, particularly outside Bavaria.

The Nazi Party was riddled with divisions, personal and political. Hitler saw it as his priority to re-found the party, based on absolute obedience to his position as leader. The finer points of policy could be ignored. There was to be no debate on the *25 Points*. The question was not to be raised of how socialist the Nazi Party was. On 24 February 1925 a mass inaugural meeting was held in Munich. Hitler spoke for 2 hours and his Bavarian sidekicks — who had been quarrelling bitterly among themselves — now swore loyalty to their leader and to the party. Munich was to continue as the site of the NSDAP headquarters. Hitler resisted all attempts to move it further north. But a real tension continued between the Bavarian headquarters of the party and the branches in northern Germany.

Hitler was also determined to bring the SA under greater control. This led to the resignation of Röhm and his replacement by Captain Franz von Pfeffer, a more amenable tool. A northern group of politicians, centred around **Gregor Strasser** and **Josef Goebbels**, was anxious to emphasise the socialist nature of the NSDAP. In foreign policy these men stressed the possibilities of cooperation with Bolshevik Russia and demanded a party commitment against the wealth and privileges of the former German princes. Hitler totally outmanoeuvred this group at a conference held at Bamberg in February 1926 by packing the meeting with his southern supporters. The young Goebbels was appalled, recording in his diary, 'I no longer believe fully in Hitler'. Yet 2 months later Hitler charmed him, winning him over totally. This time Goebbels wrote in his diary, 'Adolf Hitler, I love you because you are both great and simple at the same time'. Strasser was also won over and appointed propaganda chief at the end of the year. Goebbels was appointed party **Gauleiter** of Berlin, with the task of winning the capital for the NSDAP. Hitler's skill as a politician rested not only on his public speaking but also on his charisma and ability to manipulate other politicians.

It would be a mistake, however, to focus entirely on Hitler or even the other party bosses between 1925 and 1928. The importance of these years to the future triumph of the Nazi Party lay in the spread of 'local groups' throughout the whole of Weimar Germany. The establishment and success of these depended upon the energy and character of the individual Nazis in the area. Near Hanover, in the little town of **Northeim**, the Nazis owed much to the brutal energy of a local lad, Ernst Girmann, and the high moral character of the local bookseller, Wilhelm Spannaus — a pillar of the local community and church and one of the first to join the Nazi Party in the town. Many felt that if the Nazi Party was good enough for Spannaus, then it was good enough for them. Across Germany, party membership grew steadily from 27,000 at the end of 1925 to 108,000 in 1928. Although the typical party member was likely to be lower-middle-class and young, the party — unlike others — did transcend class and religious boundaries.

The task of the local group was propaganda, whether through pamphlets, meetings or face-to-face confrontation. From top to bottom the party appreciated the need to go out and convert, a feature that marked it almost as a religious movement. Money always remained a problem. Each local group had to fund its own activities as well as make a contribution to party headquarters in Munich. Subordinate special groups were created within the party, e.g. the National Socialist Union of University Students. A youth branch was created in 1926, when the words Hitler Youth appeared for the first time.

What was created between 1925 and 1928 was a formidable modern party political machine that could, when the time was right, capture political power. Unfortunately for Hitler and the Nazi Party, the time was not right. In the 1928 Reichstag election it gained only 810,000 votes and a mere 12 seats. This poor performance brought one unlooked-for blessing. Hitler's public speaking ban was lifted in Prussia and most other German states.

Glossary and concepts

Gauleiter — regional Nazi Party boss. Gauleiters have often been likened to medieval barons, enjoying wide local independence in return for their unconditional loyalty to the party leader.

Northeim — small town in central north Germany, near to Hanover and the subject of an excellent detailed study by the American William Sheridan Allen, who published his findings in a book entitled *The Nazi Seizure of Power* (1965, Franklin Watts, New York).

Key figures

Josef Goebbels (1897–1945) — a clever intellectual from a working-class Catholic background in western Germany. He joined the NSDAP in 1924 and was completely won over by Hitler's personality in 1926. Hitler sent him to Berlin to win the capital for the Nazis. He failed, but impressed many with his courage and energy. He was placed in charge of party propaganda in 1929 and masterminded the Nazi breakthrough in the election of September 1930. After Hitler came to power he was appointed Minister of Enlightenment and Propaganda, a post he held until 1945. He committed suicide with his wife and six children at the same time as Hitler.

Gregor Strasser (1892–1934) — joined the Nazi Party in the early 1920s and took part in the Munich Putsch. He became leader of the north German wing of the party and favoured more radical, socialist policies. He was the original patron of Goebbels. He was an excellent administrator, and the second most important person in the party to Hitler until their quarrel in 1932. He withdrew from active politics but was murdered in 1934 in the Night of the Long Knives.

Gustav Stresemann (1878–1929) — leader of the DVP and a key figure in enabling the Weimar Republic to prosper during the years 1924 to 1929. During these 5 years he was Foreign Minister and massively improved Germany's standing in the world. He was also crucial in holding together various coalitions. His death in October 1929 was a disaster for democracy in Germany.

The Nazi breakthrough to power, 1929–33

The death throes of the Weimar Republic

Most people associated the economic crisis that struck Germany in 1929 with the Wall Street Crash of October of that year. In fact the German economy was already in serious trouble. Agriculture in particular had been struggling for years. Over 13 million people owed their livelihoods directly to farming: a far larger percentage of the population than was the case in Britain. Agricultural protection, which had been in place since 1879, was removed in 1924 and foreign competition began to hurt many small and less efficient farmers. Bankruptcies multiplied and debts to banks increased. Grain prices fell after 1927 and there was serious distress. Early in 1928 there were widespread demonstrations by farmers in many regions. In Oldenburg 30,000 people demonstrated. In Schleswig-Holstein the number of protesters reached 140,000 and there was widespread violence. Rural suffering was keenly felt because farmers and farm labourers were not included in the National Insurance scheme of 1927. As farm incomes collapsed, misery and hunger became widespread. This became increasingly acute as depression settled over Germany between 1930 and 1931.

In urban and industrial Germany all was not well at the beginning of 1929. At the end of 1928 there had been a bitter dispute within the Ruhr steel industry over wages. Employers felt that wages were too high and that the government arbitration system favoured the workers. Many powerful industrialists in Weimar Germany were becoming disillusioned with the system. Growth was slowing down everywhere in 1929. The flow of foreign investment was decreasing before the Wall Street Crash. The slump in the USA was doubly disastrous for Germany. The influx of capital on which Germany relied disappeared and many companies found themselves called upon to repay their debts. Exports were also hit as Germany's foreign trade collapsed. Unemployment mounted. In 1929 it stood at 2 million; by 1931 it reached 4½ million. In that year there was a series of bank collapses that added to the country's woes. By 1932 unemployment had reached nearly 6 million and even this figure understated the scale of the problem. Many in agriculture were virtually unemployed, yet the statistics did not include these. At least a third of all working Germans were without wages. This amounted to a vast tide of human misery, which showed itself in the suicide statistics of 250 per million inhabitants (compared to 85 per million in Britain). Despair and fear stalked the land. Those who were unemployed worried about where the next crust of bread was going to come from and those who still had jobs were terrified that they would join the ranks of the unemployed.

A political crisis mirrored the economic one. Like the economic crisis, its origins pre-dated the Wall Street Crash of October 1929. Party politics was being polarised, making the cooperation that was essential to coalition government increasingly difficult to achieve. The Communist Party, under orders from Moscow, saw the SPD not as its natural ally but as its bitterest enemy, a rival for the working-class vote. The KPD constantly sniped at the moderate socialists, denouncing them as class traitors. This made it harder for the SPD to work with the bourgeois parties to achieve the consensus that was necessary for good government.

In December 1928 the Centre Party also moved over to the right when Monsignor Kaas won the leadership. The DDP, perhaps the party most loyal to the republic, was fading away. On the right, the DNVP — which, although openly monarchist, had at least increasingly cooperated with the other parties — came under the leadership of **Alfred Hugenberg** in October 1928. He wished to restructure the Weimar Republic on authoritarian grounds.

The crucial figure holding together the democratic coalition government was Gustav Stresemann, the Foreign Minister. In 1929 he pulled off a major triumph when he persuaded the British and French to accept a further reduction in reparations, which became known as the **Young Plan**. The Allies also agreed to withdraw all their troops from Germany 5 years early. It was Stresemann's last diplomatic achievement, as he died suddenly on 3 October 1929 at the age of 51. This was a severe blow to the Müller coalition government. Hugenberg launched a nationwide campaign against the Young Plan — a campaign into which he drew Hitler. A national referendum was held in December 1929. Only 13% voted for Hitler and Hugenberg's call to reject the plan. Hitler did not mind the defeat, because the campaign had given him enormous press coverage.

In March 1930 the economic crisis suddenly intensified the political crisis. Government revenue fell sharply as the slump began to bite, while at the same time expenditure rose rapidly, with the need to pay welfare benefits to the unemployed. In the light of prevailing orthodox economic theory, either taxation had to rise or benefits had to be cut. The SPD and the DVP could not agree a joint course of action. The middle-class DVP insisted on benefit cuts, which the SPD would not concede. The governing coalition broke up.

No chancellor could be found who could command a majority in the Reichstag. The President, Hindenburg, appointed a member of the Catholic Centre Party, **Heinrich Brüning**, as Chancellor and agreed that he would support Brüning's rule through the use of presidential emergency decrees. Parliamentary democracy had effectively come to an end — or it was, at the very least, suspended. In an attempt to gain a majority, Brüning held Reichstag elections in September 1930. These were a disaster for moderate politics. Both the extreme right and the extreme left made significant gains. Germany seemed to be fragmenting and becoming ungovernable. Street violence increased as the slump deepened. For 2 years Brüning wrestled with an almost impossible situation. His attempt to cut government expenditure arguably made the slump worse in the short term. In 1932 he persuaded the Allies to drop all reparations, but their agreement came too late to prevent his dismissal by President Hindenburg.

Hindenburg's coolness towards Brüning sprang in part from Brüning's own miscalculations. Brüning had persuaded the ageing Hindenburg to stand for re-election as President in 1932, telling him that it would be a walkover and would require little effort. Brüning was sadly mistaken and the elections went to a second ballot when Hindenburg failed to get an overall majority in the first. Brüning and Hindenburg also argued over measures to promote agricultural reform. The President refused to sign an emergency decree dealing with bankrupt agricultural estates in eastern Germany and Brüning was forced to resign.

Following Brüning's resignation, Hindenburg was persuaded to try to establish a majority conservative coalition government, thereby escaping the need for rule by presidential decree. A key figure in conservative circles was a clever political general called **Kurt von Schleicher**. He, like many army officers, was worried that Germany would disintegrate into civil war and that the army, instead of defending Germany from its foreign enemies, would have to take to the streets and risk killing German citizens in order to restore order. The President picked a charming aristocrat from the Centre Party, **Franz von Papen**, as his new Chancellor on 1 June 1932, in the hope that von Papen could do a deal with both the DNVP and the Nazis. Hitler's price for cooperation, which von Papen agreed to pay, was another general election. The Nazi vote soared and Hitler, in a stronger position than before, refused to serve under von Papen. The street violence intensified in the autumn and in desperation von Papen called fresh elections in November. The Nazi vote fell slightly but that of the communists increased.

Von Schleicher stepped in, persuading President Hindenburg to dismiss von Papen as Chancellor. Hindenburg appointed von Schleicher to replace von Papen. Von Schleicher hoped to achieve a left-wing coalition majority government by uniting the SPD with part of the Nazi Party under Gregor Strasser. The plan failed and the government continued relying on presidential emergency decree for its legality.

Von Papen was furious with von Schleicher and determined on revenge. Von Schleicher's failure provided him with his opportunity. After weeks of complex negotiations the ancient President was prevailed upon to accept Adolf Hitler as Chancellor in a coalition government with the DNVP. The conservatives like Hugenberg and von Papen thought they were using Hitler to achieve a more authoritarian system of government. He would be their front man. They would govern. They were mistaken.

The Nazi breakthrough to power

Before 1928 the Nazi Party had been essentially an urban party drawing its support from small craftsmen and young ex-soldiers. It had set itself the task of winning over the German working class and for this reason Goebbels had been sent to Berlin. On the whole it had not succeeded by 1928, as the general election results showed.

Despite the generally poor performance, however, there were encouraging signs that the party was doing well among the distressed farming community. In Oldenburg, where there had been extensive protest demonstrations by farmers, the Nazis picked up 7.5% of the vote in the Landtag elections of May 1928. They gradually decided to shift their efforts to winning the rural vote. The interests and needs of farmers began to be addressed in Nazi propaganda and eventually, in June 1930, the party created a special section to target farmers, under Walther Darre. The party organisations created to target youth were also beginning to have an effect and the Nazis were winning over large numbers of students at universities. In the course of 1929, Hitler's astute alliance with Hugenberg in a campaign against the Young Plan provided him with access to the mass media. Hugenberg owned several newspapers and a radio and film empire. Even though the vote was lost, Hitler gained a coverage throughout Germany that he would otherwise not have had. By the end of 1929 party membership had nearly doubled to 176,000, and the party received a very encouraging result in the

Thuringia Landtag election, scoring just over 11% of the vote. As a result, for the first time, a Nazi became a regional minister. From being a fringe party that had no real political importance, the Nazis had reached a position whereby they had to be taken more seriously.

As the depression hit ever harder at Germans' pockets and self-confidence, the attraction of the Nazis increased. Farmers and young voters seem to have been particularly susceptible to the Nazi message. What marked the Nazi Party out was its appeal to all social groups and all religions, though it did less well in the traditional urban working-class centres and devout Catholic areas loyal to the Centre Party. Nonetheless, it did attract many workers and many Catholics. It could claim to be a truly national party and this was an essential part of its appeal. It promised to restore the unity after which many Germans hankered. It looked back to the spirit of 1914 and denounced the November Criminals of 1918. Jews, Marxists and the Treaty of Versailles were the stock-in-trade villains of the Nazis. They offered no precise solutions to the slump, simply asserting that the Weimar system had failed and should be replaced.

The evidence of Nazi popularity in the Saxony Landtag election was confirmed when Brüning mistakenly called a general election in September 1930. Hitler's party did spectacularly well, gaining 18% of the vote and 107 Reichstag seats. The Nazis became the second biggest party after the SPD. A return to democratic parliamentary government, which is what Brüning had hoped to achieve, was now almost impossible. In Northeim the Nazi vote increased from 123 to 1,742, 28% of the electorate. Of these, nearly half were new voters, either newly qualified or voters who had not bothered to vote before. Hitler was now a major national politician.

Street violence escalated as brutal confrontations between the NSDAP supporters and the communists became ever more frequent. The Nazis sought the communists out and made a hero out of Horst Wessel, who was shot in 1930 by a communist gunman. According to the communists, the killing arose from an argument over a retired prostitute, but Goebbels turned Horst Wessel into a religious martyr in the obituary that appeared in his paper, *Der Angriff*. Wessel, an SA man, had composed a battle song in 1929 and this now became the hymn of the Nazi movement.

The numbers in the SA grew dramatically in line with the economic crisis. Early in 1931 it had 88,000 members. By the end of the year it had 260,000. The relationship between the party and the SA had never been easy. It required considerable skill on Hitler's part to maintain control. Many SA men resented the party bureaucrats at Gau headquarters. They wanted to return to the violence of 1923, preferring a head-on assault on the Weimar Republic to the creeping pace of the ballot box.

In 1930 Hitler had been forced to take over the leadership of the SA himself to restore some sort of control over the Berlin SA organisation. A further crisis developed in 1931 — generally referred to as **Stennes' Revolt**. Walther Stennes was the leader of the SA in the eastern regions of Germany. Hitler had already tried to increase the loyalty of the SA by recalling Ernst Röhm as Chief of Staff in January 1930. Stennes' resentment, both of Hitler's leadership and his pursuit of the parliamentary path to power, led to open rebellion and attacks on Hitler in a party paper. Hitler fought back with considerable skill, offering the SA men of Berlin a choice between Stennes, a retired police sergeant, and himself, the potential saviour of Germany. Hitler emerged triumphant and restored Goebbels' authority in Berlin over a purged SA. Throughout 1931 and 1932 Hitler was forced into a very delicate balancing act. He had to keep the radicals of the SA happy with promises of change but he also had to keep the flood of new middle-class Nazi voters happy with promises of stability and order. It was to reassure the middle class that Hitler formed a tactical alliance in the autumn of 1931 with Alfred Hugenberg of the DNVP and Franz Seldte, head of the veterans association, the **Stahlhelm** ('Steel Helmet'). This alliance was known as the National Opposition, or the **Harzburg Front**, on account of a massive rally held on 11 October at Bad Harzburg. Such flirtations with the conservative right were disliked by the radicals of the SA and the party. It was one of Hitler's greatest political achievements that he was able to persuade large numbers of Germans that the Nazis were both a party of the right and a party of the left. By the spring of 1932 membership of the party had reached 1 million. It was an astonishing achievement in such a short time.

Elections were commonplace in 1932: there were two for the presidency in the spring, regional elections and two elections for the Reichstag. In the presidential elections Hitler felt strong enough to challenge Hindenburg for the presidency. Hitler forced a second ballot, which the old Field Marshal only won with the support of the SPD and the Centre Party — support he resented. Hitler gained 13 million votes in all and won the support of large numbers of middle-class conservative voters. Elections kept the country in a ferment of political activity and violence. The Nazis caused much of the latter, but posed as the party which could stop it. The growing strength of the communists frightened middle-class voters, leading many to the Nazi Party as the lesser of two evils.

Following the violence carried out by the SA in the presidential elections, the new government successfully banned the SA. Hitler was forced to choose humiliating submission, hateful to the radicals in his party, or military confrontation with the government, which he knew he would lose. This was a major setback but, as on other occasions, circumstances came to Hitler's rescue. First the Minister of Defence, responsible for the ban on the SA, was sacked by the President. Then the Chancellor, Brüning, was replaced by von Papen. The new Chancellor sought to gain Hitler's support in order to achieve a majority in the Reichstag. Hitler played his hand well. He hinted that cooperation would be forthcoming if fresh elections were held and the ban on the SA was lifted. Hitler got his way.

The result was an electoral triumph for the Nazis. They won nearly 37% of the vote. The result was the product of many factors. Hitler was certainly a star turn, moving rapidly from town to town in whistle-stop tours. Goebbels was a propagandist of genius. But it was not merely the Nazi leaders who were responsible for success. In many towns and villages which had never seen Hitler the voters turned out in their hundreds and thousands to vote for the Nazis. It was the local Nazi stalwarts who brought in these voters. The Nazis were now the biggest party in Germany and, quite understandably, Hitler demanded to be made Chancellor. The President refused to consider such a proposition. Hitler was not a gentleman. He belonged on the wilder extremes of politics and would, Hindenburg feared, destabilise Germany further if he became Chancellor. There was stalemate.

Von Papen continued as Chancellor with an even smaller number of Reichstag votes behind him than Brüning. In desperation, in November 1932, he persuaded the President to call a further Reichstag election. The Nazi Party was, as usual, strapped for cash. Already there were the first signs of recovery in the economy; possibly Hitler was too late. The election showed a real fall in support and the number of Nazi MPs reduced from 230 to 196. But Communist Party support increased to 17%. This was to help Hitler. Fear of the Communist Party led many of the old élite, who intrinsically disliked Hitler, to accept him as a necessary evil. Such was probably the view of Hindenburg.

November was the make-or-break month for the future Führer. General von Schleicher tried to break up the Nazi Party and win over a large segment of its MPs under Gregor Strasser. Hitler was deeply depressed but Strasser refused to join a government without Hitler's blessing. The result was that von Schleicher continued to rely on the President's emergency decrees. He was, in fact, rapidly losing the President's confidence and that of the other senior generals in the army. They were increasingly worried at the prospect of civil war and wanted a chancellor with a majority. It was in these circumstances that Hitler was brought into government, just as his support was beginning to fail. Von Papen persuaded the President to appoint Hitler as Chancellor with himself as Vice Chancellor. The majority of the Cabinet were not Nazis. Von Papen and Hugenberg, Minister of Economics, thought they had captured Hitler for their own purposes. They would use him. The army gave the government its blessing. Only two other ministers were Nazis, but one of these controlled the police. The wild celebrating by the SA and party supporters on that night of 30 January 1933 should have given von Papen and the other conservatives cause for concern.

Glossary and concepts

Harzburg Front — loose political alliance of the NSDAP, DNVP and the *Stahlhelm* against the Brüning government in 1931. This seemed to align the Nazis with the conservative forces in Germany and was much criticised by radical Nazis, who took the socialist element in the party seriously.

Stahlhelm — association of First World War veteran soldiers, led by Franz Seldte.

Stennes' Revolt — challenge to Hitler's authority and that of Goebbels in Berlin in 1931 by a group of SA men led by Walther Stennes. He and the SA men resented the attempt to control their violence, which Hitler feared would upset the middle class, which was increasingly coming over to the Nazi Party. Tension remained despite Hitler's victory, a tension that was not to be resolved until the Night of the Long Knives in 1934.

Young Plan — scheme negotiated by Gustav Stresemann just before his death (in 1929) for the reduction of reparations payments. It was a major diplomatic success, but to the nationalist forces of the NSDAP and the DNVP it was a reminder of the humiliation of Versailles. The two parties formed an alliance to reject the scheme following a national referendum. The campaign against the Young Plan gave Hitler valuable media coverage, even though the referendum was lost.

Key figures

Heinrich Brüning (1885–1970) — served as an officer in the First World War and became an MP in 1924 for the Catholic Centre Party. He became Chancellor in March 1930 but had no majority in Parliament and had to rely on presidential decrees. He tried to cut government expenditure and this possibly added to unemployment. He was dismissed by the President just as he had seen through the worst of the slump. When Hitler came to power he left Germany and emigrated to the USA.

Alfred Hugenberg (1865–1951) — rich German politician who controlled a vast media empire. He was a nationalist and opposed to the Weimar Republic. This led him to cooperate with the NSDAP in 1929, 1931 and in Hitler's government of 1933. He resigned from this government in June and thereafter played little part in politics.

Franz von Papen (1879–1969) — a Roman Catholic aristocrat and soldier, he was appointed Chancellor in 1932 in the hope of producing a right-wing coalition government with a majority. He failed to do a deal with Hitler in the summer of 1932 but eventually played a vital part in bringing Hitler to power in January 1933. He served as Vice Chancellor until 1934 but then lost power and was sent as ambassador to Vienna.

Kurt von Schleicher (1882–1934) — a professional soldier who became the political liaison officer of the army High Command. In 1932 he had considerable influence over the President and passed on the concerns of many generals about civil war and the dangers of the army being dragged into it. He tried on two occasions to produce a majority government and in both cases failed. His failure opened the way for Hitler to come to power, but he never lost his taste for intrigue. This caused him to be shot in June 1934.

The consolidation of power, January–March 1933

From Chancellor to Führer

Hitler had become Chancellor on 30 January 1933. He was not, however, a dictator. He could be dismissed at any time by the President, and a majority of his Cabinet colleagues were not of his party. In many ways his appointment as Chancellor marked a return to democracy. It was yet another attempt to return to a government that could enjoy majority support in Parliament rather than depending on emergency presidential decree. The situation had changed dramatically by the end of March 1933, when it was clear that Hitler was not merely the dupe of those conservative politicians who had 'levered him into power'. Hitler's consolidation of power was not, of course, complete in March. His policy of **Gleichschaltung** (coordination) would extend up to and beyond August 1934, when Hitler combined the roles of Chancellor and President.

Inevitably, the focus of most narratives tends to be on Hitler and events in Berlin, but it should be noted that the consolidation going on at ground level in every town and region of Germany was just as important. Thousands of local enthusiasts strengthened the Nazi hold on town halls and regional government. It was this popular dynamic that made the consolidation of power so effective and made it impossible for the conservatives around Hitler in Berlin to resist.

Hitler's first move was to persuade the President to accept another election, which was fixed for March 1933. Hitler reassured the army chiefs in a meeting on 3 February. He promised them money for rearmament and — most important for the majority of them — their independence from politics. They would not be called upon to deal with the communists and could be allowed to focus on the business of expansion and rearmament. Many of the generals found Hitler vulgar, but they accepted the deal. General von Blomburg, as Minister of War, was reassuring to them. On 20 February another important meeting was held with the chiefs of industry, who were reassured that capitalism was safe under the Nazis — in fact even safer than before, for Marxists would be dealt with. At the end of the meeting 3 million marks were promised for the election campaign. Perhaps even more important than these deals with the rich and powerful was the insidious perversion of the police. Already in 1932, under von Papen, a purge of senior police officers had begun. Now, under Goering and Frick, this was carried much further. On 17 February Goering urged the police to cooperate with the SA and use every form of violence against the communists, including firearms. On 22 February 50,000 SA men were drafted into the police as auxiliaries. The police would no longer be neutral when it came to breaking up demonstrations and political meetings.

The political temperature was dramatically raised on the evening of 27 February 1933, when the Reichstag building burst into flames as a result of an arson attack by the 24-year-old Dutchman Marinus van der Lubbe. Van der Lubbe had once been a communist, and the Nazi leaders chose to believe that this was all part of a great communist plot to seize power. The blaze at the Parliament building, they claimed, was the signal for a communist uprising. There has been much debate among historians about this event. Some have tried to show that it was organised by the Nazis, but most modern research indicates that it was a fortuitous event that played into Hitler's hands. He and the other Nazi leaders appeared to be genuinely surprised by the blaze and acted as if they believed a Bolshevik seizure of power was imminent. Given Hitler's obsession with the communist rising in Munich in 1919, his outrage was probably genuine. The importance of this event lies in the use that was made of it. The President was persuaded to issue an emergency decree on 28 February 'for the protection of people and state'. Personal liberties were suspended and wide powers of arrest were granted to the government. The powers of the regional governments could be overridden. By the end of March 25,000 had been arrested in Prussia alone. The detainees were mainly communists, but some members of the SPD were also arrested. Many of the detained communists were held in temporary prisons where they were brutally tortured. The way had been opened for dictatorship.

In this frenzied atmosphere the last democratic elections in Weimar Germany were held on 5 March 1933. Despite the intimidation and the weighty government propaganda orchestrated by Goebbels, the government enjoyed only limited success. The Nazi vote rose to nearly 44%, which, together with the 8% for the DNVP, gave the government a clear majority. The result, though, was far short of the two-thirds majority that Hitler expected and needed to alter the constitution. As it happened, this did not matter. SA violence multiplied. To many it seemed Germany had been given over to hooligans. Party activists seized power throughout the country. Everywhere the Nazis took over the regional and city governments. In Bavaria, as was appropriate for the home of the movement, particularly vicious and enthusiastic Nazis gained control. Himmler, the head of the **Schutzstaffel** (SS), Hitler's personal bodyguard, became police chief and outdid Goering in his enthusiasm for the arrest and re-education of opponents of the regime.

Between 21 and 23 March 1933 three crucial developments signalled the future that awaited Germany. On 21 March a solemn piece of propaganda theatre was played out at Potsdam, the little town outside Berlin that has always been associated with the glories of Frederick the Great. President Hindenburg, in the full uniform of a Prussian field marshal, partnered the new Reich Chancellor in a ceremony of national reconciliation and awakening. Old and new were to be bound together, creating the **Volksgemeinschaft**. The next day, far to the south in Bavaria, a new institution opened for the first time — Dachau, Himmler's new model concentration camp. It was a name that was to strike terror into many Germans over the next 12 years. On 23 March, at the first meeting of the new Reichstag in the Kroll Opera House in Berlin, the German Parliament passed what has become known as the Enabling Act. Its official name was the 'Act for the Removal of Distress from the People and the Reich'. After much debate the Centre Party agreed to support the Nazi Party, hoping to preserve the influence of the Catholic Church in the new Germany. Only 94 brave SPD deputies voted against the Bill. The Parliament transferred its authority for 4 years to the Chancellor. Weimar Germany had committed suicide.

Conclusions

Historians have argued for years over the fate of the Weimar Republic and the reasons for the triumph of Adolf Hitler. In postwar communist East Germany the standard explanation was that Hitler was merely the tool of threatened capitalists. Big business had put Hitler into power to crush the workers. In West Germany it was fashionable to explain the triumph of the Nazis in terms of Hitler's charismatic powers. It was as if Hitler had bewitched the country, and it is impossible to ignore his role. He was in many ways a politician of genius, an outstanding speaker, a superb manipulator of others; he also possessed a crucial sense of timing. Alongside Hitler, Goebbels must rank as one of the great propagandists of all time. Hitler certainly appreciated Goebbels' talents and he deserves much of the credit for the Nazi breakthrough in the election of 1930, which he managed for the party.

Yet the actions of these outstanding individuals do not explain the transformation of the Nazi Party between 1928, when it was little more than a fringe organisation, and 1932, when it had become a mass party. Clearly the economic slump and attendant misery created the right conditions for breakthrough. Poverty-stricken unemployed workers joined the Nazis in the hope of a better world. So did the young in their thousands; so did the peasants and so did the middle class, fearful of the Communist Party. The Nazi Party and Hitler filled a void that had been growing since the nineteenth century. It offered faith and hope to a world where traditional religion seemed less and less relevant. It was in many ways an alternative religious cult — with Hitler a cult leader. It offered order to a country which had lost its Kaiser. It offered redemption to a Germany which had been humiliated in 1919 and seen its currency disappear in 1923. The old world had been mocked in the 1920s by the radical artists and dramatists of the Weimar Republic but, in destroying the remnants of the old world, they had prepared the ground for new beliefs and new icons.

Ordinary Germans put Hitler into power. Large numbers never voted for him, but he was a popular politician who enjoyed support throughout all classes and regions of the country. Intelligence and education offered no immunity. The Nazi Party was filled with doctors of philosophy. Like most religions and cults, the Nazis' success had a strong theatrical element. The young Hitler had been obsessed with Wagner's grandiose operas. He saw himself in a Wagnerian role, saving Germany from Jewish and Marxist monsters. If only more Germans had laughed at the fantasy; Hitler was morbidly frightened of ridicule and perhaps secretly sensed his vulnerability. Not enough Germans laughed, but then there was little to make them laugh in 1932.

Glossary and concepts

Gleichschaltung (coordination) — the Nazification of German political and social institutions. At the higher level this refers to the taking over of the *Länder*, or state governments, but it could involve the Nazification of, for example, a town choir or chess club, as happened in Northeim.

Schutzstaffel (SS) — originally a branch of the SA, the SS was founded in 1925 to protect leading Nazis at meetings. The uniform was black and not brown (as with the SA). Himmler was appointed its commander in 1929 and built it into the most formidable of all the subordinate organisations of Nazi Germany.

Volksgemeinschaft (racial folk community) — term to describe the vision of a harmonious Germany, devoid of class tensions and 'racial impurities'.

Questions
&
Answers

In this section there are five specimen exam questions. They illustrate the range and type of source extracts you will come across.

Two specimen answers are given to each exam question. One of these is an A-grade answer, but examples of lower-grade answers are included to point out common errors — either in approach or in exam technique.

All the specimen answers are the subject of detailed examiner comments, preceded by the icon *e*. These should be studied carefully as they show how and why marks are awarded or lost. They demonstrate common features in A-grade answers such as:
- the appropriate use of outside knowledge to put source material in context
- a clear and persistent focus on answering the question asked
- a structured and logical approach
- an apportionment of time and effort within answers appropriate to marks that can be gained in different parts of the question

When exam papers are marked, all answers are given a level of response and then a precise numerical mark. Answers to questions worth 10 marks are normally marked to three levels:
- **level 1:** 1–4 marks
- **level 2:** 5–8 marks
- **level 3:** 9–10 marks

The final essay is marked to four levels:
- **level 1:** 1–6 marks, involves very simple statements and the use of either own knowledge or information from one extract
- **level 2:** 7–12 marks, involves either own knowledge and limited source use, or excellent use of the sources alone, or excellent own knowledge
- **level 3:** 13–18 marks, involves using both sources and own knowledge with real focus on the question asked
- **level 4:** 19–24 marks, involves a sustained argument from both the sources and own knowledge

Question 1

Source 1: *From an account of a Nazi meeting in 1932 written at the time by a Hamburg school teacher*

When this speech was over, there was roaring enthusiasm and applause. Hitler saluted, gave his thanks, the Horst Wessel song sounded out across the course. Hitler was helped into his coat. Then he went — how many look up to him with a touching faith! As their helper, a saviour, their deliverer from unbearable distress — to him who rescues the Prussian prince, the scholar, the clergyman, the farmer, the worker, the unemployed, who rescues them, from the parties back into the nation.

Source 2: *From* Inside the Third Reich *by Albert Speer, later one of Hitler's ministers. He is writing about 1931 but the book was written many years later in the 1960s*

It must have been during these months that my mother saw an SA parade in the streets of Heidelberg. The sight of discipline in a time of chaos, the impression of energy in an atmosphere of universal hopelessness, seems to have won her over also. At any rate, without ever having heard a speech or read a pamphlet she joined the party. Both of us seem to have felt this decision to be a breach with a liberal family tradition. In any case we concealed it from one another and from my father. Only years later, long after I had become a part of Hitler's inner circle, did my mother and I discover by chance that we shared an early membership in the party.

Source 3: *Chancellors of the Weimar Republic, 1919–33, with names of parties forming the government*

Scheidemann, February–June 1919 (SPD, Centre, DDP)
Bauer, June 1919–March 1920 (SPD, Centre, DDP)
Müller, March–June 1920 (SPD, DDP, Centre)
Fehrenbach, June 1920–May 1921 (DDP, Centre, DVP)
Wirth, May–October 1921 (SPD, DDP, Centre)
Wirth, October 1921–November 1922 (SPD, DDP, Centre)
Cuno, November 1922–August 1923 (DDP, Centre, DVP)
Stresemann, August–October 1923 (SPD, DDP, Centre, DVP)
Stresemann, October–November 1923 (SPD to 3 November, DDP, Centre, DVP)
Marx, November 1923–June 1924 (DDP, Centre, BVP, DVP)
Marx, June 1924–January 1925 (DDP, Centre, DVP)
Luther, January–December 1925 (Centre, DVP, DNVP, BVP)
Luther, January–May 1926 (Centre, DDP, DVP, BVP)

1

question

Marx, May–December 1926 (DDP, Centre, DVP, BVP)
Marx, January 1927–June 1928 (Centre, DVP, DNVP, BVP)
Müller, June 1928–March 1930 (SPD, DDP, Centre, BVP, DVP)
Brüning, March 1930–October 1931 (Presidential Cabinet)
Brüning, October 1931–May 1932 (Presidential Cabinet)
Von Papen, June–December 1932 (Presidential Cabinet)
Von Schleicher, December 1932–January 1933 (Presidential Cabinet)
Hitler, January 1933

Source 4: *From* Hitler and Nazi Germany *by Stephen J. Lee, 1998*

The rise of Hitler depended directly on the vulnerability of the Weimar Republic. Although in many respects an advanced democracy, the Republic was politically flawed and susceptible to economic crisis. There were practical difficulties arising out of the constitution. Proportional representation, without a threshold, produced a multiplicity of parties, encouraged splinter groups and made coalition governments inevitable, with all the potential for internal disagreement which these so often carry. This was made worse at certain points in the history of the republic by economic crises, especially those of 1921–23 and 1929–31. The collapse of democracy in 1929 was due to the interaction of the two processes. The Great Coalition which comprised the Social Democratic Party (SPD), the Centre, the People's Party (DVP) and the Democratic Party (DDP) — was already in disarray before 1929 but was brought down by the disagreement between the SPD and the Centre for proposals to cut unemployment benefit. The results were the decline of party politics and the growth of authoritarian government with less and less recourse to the Reichstag. As will be seen, this was an ideal situation for the Nazi Party.

(a) **Study Source 4**
  What, according to this source, were the reasons for the collapse of democracy in 1929 in Weimar Germany? (6 marks)
(b) **Use your own knowledge to explain what the SA was.** (10 marks)
(c) **Study Sources 3 and 4**
  What evidence in Source 3 supports the views expressed in Source 4 about the nature of the Weimar Constitution? (10 marks)
(d) **Study Sources 1 and 2**
  How useful are these two sources to a historian studying the appeal of the Nazi Party to voters in 1931–32? (10 marks)
(e) **Study Sources 2 and 4 and use your own knowledge**
  How important was the economic crisis of 1929–33 in explaining the growth in support for the Nazi Party? (24 marks)

■ ■ ■

Answer to question 1: candidate A

(a) According to Source 4, the collapse of democracy in 1929 was largely due to two contributory factors: economic crisis and political instability. The two converged in 1929 in peculiar circumstances, which destroyed the coalition government. Weimar Germany had operated on a system of proportional representation which led to the formation of many different parties and necessitated coalition governments that were inherently unstable and prone to division. The acute economic crisis of 1929–31 led to disagreement over the issue of unemployment, with the result that the Great Coalition collapsed over proposals to cut unemployment benefit. A more authoritarian form of government, ruling increasingly without the Reichstag, emerged in its place, resulting in the decline of democratic party politics and the rise of the Nazi Party.

(b) The SA (*Sturmabteilung* or 'storm division'), more commonly known as 'brownshirts', served as the paramilitary arm of the Nazi Party. They were founded in 1921 and operated under the command of Ernst Röhm. They were a crucial element in the rise of the Nazi Party, intimidating and attacking opponents and forming the Nazi parades which presented an impressive spectacle of order and discipline. Once Hitler obtained power, however, they found themselves with no clear role. Hitler then made a decisive strike against them in the Night of the Long Knives in 1934, which effectively curbed their power.

(c) Source 4 asserts that there were 'practical difficulties' arising out of the Weimar Constitution. This was largely a result of proportional representation which created many parties and splinter groups within the Reichstag. As it was extremely unlikely that any party would ever gain an overall majority, governments were, by necessity, formed through coalition. They were therefore constantly prone to internal disagreement and collapse. Source 3 shows a list of Weimar chancellors between 1919 and 1933 — alongside the parties comprising the coalition government at the time. It supports the ideas expressed in Source 4, in that it illustrates that a government, and particularly a Chancellor, often lasted little more than a few months. Indeed, there were 20 Chancellors in only 14 years. This obviously suggests unstable government, constant disagreement and a lack of coherent policy. Only Müller and the Great Coalition of 1928–30, which consisted of five different parties, existed for almost 2 years. Brüning lasted a similar length of time, but under a far more authoritarian government controlled by Presidential Cabinet. As Source 4 asserts, therefore, the Weimar Constitution posed real practical difficulties, as the Weimar government clearly exhibited constant fluctuation and inconstancy.

(d) Sources 1 and 2 obviously have their uses for the historian, but it is important also to be aware of their limitations. Source 1 is the opinion of one man and is indicative of individual bias. It cannot, for example, be deduced that all Hamburg school teachers looked favourably upon the Nazi Party, as he clearly did. Nevertheless, the account was written at the time, and is therefore less likely to be clouded by failing memory. It also appears to be reflective of real heart-felt sentiments, and as long these are not used to draw inaccurate generalisations, such an extract could be valuable. That Hitler could have induced such a positive response in anyone is important for the historian to recognise. It may provide some insight into Hitler's popular appeal. The author writes: 'how many look up to him with a touching faith!', suggesting that while this passage may be the words of one individual, many more may indeed have felt as he did. He develops this idea as he goes on to recall the broad base of Hitler's support, which may contain more than a smattering of exaggeration in listing everyone from the Prussian prince to the unemployed. (Hitler failed, for example, to gain substantial support from the unemployed.) Nevertheless, it suggests that Hitler's appeal was far-reaching, going beyond the pull of factional parties and appealing to a common nation. Source 2 is written by Albert Speer, who became one of Hitler's inner circle and published this book retrospectively. It is, therefore, unsurprisingly pro-Nazi. Speer claims that both he and his mother joined the Nazi Party in its early days. It would clearly be in Speer's personal interests to justify himself as an early supporter of Hitler, and to prove that his close family were of similar sentiments. His claims could therefore be dubious. He also claims to understand his mother's feelings and reasons for joining, which could easily be inaccurate and fabricated to explain his own standing and paint the Nazis in a favourable light. Nevertheless, he writes of the impressive sight of the SA parade, which represented 'energy' and 'discipline in a time of chaos'. This offers some indication of Nazi appeal, and when corroborated by photographs and films of Nazi rallies and parades, and by anecdotal evidence, such as Source 1, it shows the pro-Nazi feeling their spectacles could induce.

(e) The economic crisis of 1929–33 was clearly a factor in the growth of Nazi support, largely in that it weakened the existing government and led to a political crisis. However, it was not the only reason for the increasing appeal of the Nazi Party.

The economic crisis, beginning in 1929, posed serious difficulties for Chancellor Müller and the coalition government in power. The slow economic recovery from the dark days of hyperinflation in the early 1920s was rapidly reversed as the cash from the USA which was backing this recovery dried up. Banks closed, industrial production fell by 42%, and the farming community was hit particularly hard. Unemployment rose dramatically and continued to do so, reaching nearly 30% by 1932. As Source 4 indicates, such economic difficulties had political consequences. Budgetary arguments split the coalition, which was brought down over disagreements about the cutting of unemployment benefit. The political climate was therefore one of fragmentation and disarray, while the economic slump impacted on the daily lives of the population.

This general climate perhaps made people look upon the order and apparent dynamism of the Nazi Party with favour, as Source 2 indicates. The exhibition of 'energy in an atmosphere of universal hopelessness' can only have benefited the Nazis. In terms of electoral breakdown, however, it is more difficult to see the direct effects of the economic crisis on voters. It was most obvious among rural peasant farmers, who comprised an important 30% of the population. They had suffered as a result of agricultural depression and threw their support behind the Nazis. In 1932, Hitler also made a concerted effort to court big business, with the result that its leading figures came to regard him as the man to restore order and economic equilibrium. Surprisingly, however, Hitler failed to gather the support of the vast majority of the unemployed and had similarly unspectacular success with industrial workers. These groups continued, in general, to remain loyal to the Communist Party.

The economic crisis alone cannot explain the large increase in Nazi support. The political effects of the crisis were also a result of weaknesses in the Weimar Constitution, as Source 4 indicates. The Great Coalition was not united enough to deal with the economic crisis and maintain stable government. President Hindenburg and many conservatives came to believe that more authoritarian government was required and by 1933 had decided that Hitler, as Chancellor, could provide what was needed. Their support can therefore be traced back not only to the economic crisis but to the unstable nature of Weimar governments.

However, it is important to recognise the strengths of the Nazi Party and Hitler in particular. The increase in Nazi support was a result not only of a negative response to unfavourable circumstances but also a result of positive Nazi action. The Nazi Party launched a particularly vigorous campaign in the countryside where they successfully infiltrated rural organisations and were rewarded with extensive support. Nazi scaremongering and tireless campaigns against the communists were also successful in luring a large proportion of the middle classes into the fold. The Nazis could offer law and order in the face of the communist threat, and a return to a golden era — before the instability of the Weimar Republic. First-time voters and the young also responded to the Nazi rallying cry. The Nazis were new, untainted with failure and possessed an 'energy', as mentioned in Source 2, which had great appeal. Hitler's own personal appeal should also be emphasised. His tremendous oratorical ability and shrewd political rhetoric helped cement the broad Nazi appeal. Thus, while he may have been helped by the economic crisis and the political situation it provoked, Hitler was able to seize opportunities and ensure that his hand, along with the hand of fate, was instrumental in the rapid expansion of Nazi support.

e This is a high-quality answer — it is well written, well informed and focuses on the question asked. Overall an A grade would be awarded.

The response to part (a) would be awarded full marks, 6 out of 6.

The response to part (b) is accurate and concise. It should, however, have explained the constant tension that existed between the party organisation and the SA. Part of Hitler's real political skill was his ability to manage these two branches of the Nazi organisation. The Night of the Long Knives, in 1934, was forced upon a reluctant Hitler but came at the end of years of tension. This response would secure 8 out of 10 marks.

question

The answer to part (c) would gain 8 out of 10 as well. Perhaps it should have noted that Source 3 confirms the assertion in Source 4 about the number of parties. This should have been done immediately after the second sentence in the answer. Always remember to integrate the two sources in these comparison questions. Do not simply summarise one source and then summarise the other.

The answer to part (d) is very good and would be worth full marks, although it is possibly a little long. The guidelines for level 3 responses state: 'Developed explanation well balanced between the sources and offering a clear assessment of utility grounded in understanding of content and of provenance.'

Part (e) is worth 24 marks and therefore the response needs to be given much more time than the others. This answer would be awarded level 4: 21 marks. On the whole it maintains focus on the question and integrates the sources and the candidate's own knowledge well, picking up on the key points in both sources. It could be criticised for underestimating Hitler's appeal to the unemployed and the working class and, more seriously, for failing to bring out the amazing jump in Nazi electoral support between 1928 and 1930. It also implies that the working class was essentially loyal to the Communist Party, when the majority tended to vote SPD. Nevertheless, it is a high-quality answer which matches the rest of the response and would merit an A grade.

■ ■ ■

Answer to question 1: candidate B

(a) The decline of democracy in 1929 in Weimar Germany occurred for a series of reasons. A part of the problem was Hindenburg's use of article 48, which granted him great power and undermined democracy. This was not helped by the tradition of authority that existed before Weimar Germany, since people held onto a faith in strong leadership. Also the political system of proportional representation undermined democracy because it led to coalition governments. Besides this there was a big economic problem in Weimar Germany in the late 1920s when America called in loans organised under Gustav Stresemann, therefore damaging faith in the system. Source 4 points out the problem with coalition governments, wedded to the economic crisis which provided a good basis for the Nazis' success.

(b) The SA were men in brown shirts who Hitler employed aggressively to enforce the strength of the party. They were used by Hitler in the Munich Putsch and during the Nazi rise to power to frighten people, but were then attacked later in the Night of the Long Knives, because Hitler felt threatened by their leader Ernst Röhm.

(c) Source 3 gives a list of Chancellors of the Weimar Republic between 1919 and 1933 and shows that throughout the whole period of the Weimar Republic every government was a coalition of at least three parties. It also shows how the republic gradually became more right-wing. In the early 1920s the biggest parties were the SPD and the Centre, but by the late 1920s the nationalists became more powerful, until Brüning (a nationalist) eventually took over. Source 4 shows how the Weimar Constitution was politically flawed with the system of proportional representation leading to coalition governments, making efficient government of the country difficult. It also explains how the DVP and the DDP, which formed the Great Coalition, was broken by the disagreement over cutting unemployment benefit. This, it argues, then paved the way for the Nazis. In this way Source 3 does support Source 4 since it shows the growth of the right wing just as the DVP and the DDP were splitting up.

(d) Source 1 records the experience of a Hamburg schoolteacher at a Nazi meeting in 1932. It shows how important the figure of Hitler was in himself. It describes how taken in both the teacher and the crowd were with him, and how he seemed to them to be a saviour to people in all walks of life. Source 2 shows how important the discipline of the Nazi Party was when everything seemed to be in chaos. It explains that the image of authority provided a feeling of stability when chaos prevailed. In this sense it is very useful to the historian in terms of reconstructing a picture of Hitler's rise to power.

(e) The economic crisis of 1929 to 1933 in Germany grew out of the Wall Street Crash in America. As an aspect of the growth in support for the Nazi Party it is very important. Yet it alone cannot explain the Nazis' success.

Germany between 1919 and 1923 was politically fragile owing to the problem of resentment that persisted amongst the army following the end of the First World War. Also the hyperinflation of 1923 created more hostility towards the politics of the day. The impact of this instability was to live in the memory of the German nation in spite of the increased prosperity of the years 1924–29. The early years of the Weimar Constitution had other problems, which came to the fore at the end of the decade. One of these problems was that of article 48, which granted the President excessive power, and although the first President of Weimar, Friedrich Ebert, made little use of this, his successor, Hindenburg, did. Also there was a strong tradition of authoritarianism in German politics, and many hankered after a return to the prewar situation.

Nevertheless, the concerns of the German nation were temporarily reduced in the 1925–29 period when, under Gustav Stresemann, the economic problems were cured by taking out loans from America. However, a problem that exploded in 1930 was with the system of proportional representation, which led to coalition governments, as Source 4 shows. Fortunately, so long as the coalition could agree on certain matters, problems could be kept to a minimum. Yet in 1930 the most solid coalition, made of the SPD, the DVP and the Centre Party, fell apart and, from that point on, each Chancellor was chosen by Hindenburg. This happened at the same time as the German economy collapsed. Because of the Wall Street Crash this meant that no more loans could be taken, and also that those that had been taken were being recalled. Because of this, unemployment rose to 6 million by 1932 and industrial production fell by 42%. Also the economic depression affected the agricultural industry and so rural Germany was badly affected as well. No doubt because of these problems the people were looking for a solution elsewhere, their faith in the dominant parties having been destroyed. Because of this it is not surprising that the Nazi Party grew in support.

The Nazi Party's growth was also aided by the succession of Chancellors beginning with Heinrich Brüning, who, however, only made the economic situation worse by cutting public expenditure and increasing taxes. This forced Brüning to resign and Hindenburg then appointed von Papen, who destroyed the Prussian parliament, but was driven out of office through unpopularity. Hindenburg then appointed General von Schleicher who only lasted a short while, until Hindenburg decided to appoint Hitler, who was heavily backed by industrial business and the army. Part of this success was Hitler's ability to appeal to lots of different groups in society. As Source 2 shows, a central aspect of this appeal was the appearance of discipline at a time when things were in chaos. Yet Hitler was also good at appealing to the rural agricultural areas as well as big business and the army. The Nazis played on the idea of the folk community, attracting the rural classes of society. By 1932 they had moved on to attract the middle class and the upper middle class. The Nazi Party was also a young and up-to-date movement, taking advantage of modern technology and propaganda to present an image of smart, authoritarian assurance at a time of crisis.

Hence there were many things that contributed to the growth of the Nazi Party including the economic crisis. Yet the combination of events throughout Weimar Germany all played their part.

🖉 This response is not as well expressed as the other. This can be illustrated by comparing the definitions of the SA and the use of the phrase 'brownshirts' in the two answers to part (b).

The response to part (a) contains much irrelevant material, i.e. information not given in the passage requiring comprehension. The candidate makes some valid points, however, and would earn 4 out of 6 marks.

The response to part (b) contains some valid information and would be awarded 4 out of 10 marks.

The response to part (c) tends to be two summaries of the sources rather than a genuine cross-referencing of the two sources. The comparison that is made in the last sentence is largely irrelevant. This answer would gain 4 out of 10 marks.

The answer to part (d) is the weakest of all, offering limited source summaries. It would only be awarded 3 marks out of 10.

The answer to part (e) contains much accurate and relevant information but it tends to be a narrative and contains much material from outside the dates asked for in the question. Both sources are used — not incorrectly, but not as effectively as they might be. A well-informed candidate might have known that young Albert

Speer was typical of the young middle-class Germans who threw themselves so enthusiastically behind the Nazi Party. Even the more elderly Frau Speer was, in many ways, typical of the middle-class Germans who, in 1931–32, abandoned their traditional loyalties to the Liberal Party and, out of a fear of the communists, placed their hopes in Hitler. The answer would earn 12 out of 24 marks.

Overall, this would be a high D- or low C-grade answer.

Question 2

Source 1: *Report on the problems of containing the growth of Nazism in the Protestant youth movement dated 1931*

The cause which at the moment is most closely associated with the name of national socialism and with which, at a moderate estimate, certainly 70 per cent of our young people, often lacking knowledge of the facts, are in ardent sympathy, must be regarded, as far as our ranks are concerned, more as a moral than a political matter. Our young people show little political interest. Fifth formers are not really much concerned with a study of Hitler's thoughts; it is simply something irrational, something infectious that makes the blood pulse through one's veins and conveys an impression of something great underway; the roaring of a stream which one does not wish to escape; 'if you can't feel it you will never grasp it'.

Source 2: *Complaints from November 1930 about the behaviour of Nazi school children*

Leaflets have recently been distributed in the playgrounds of the schools of the city of Oldenburg and its vicinity, inviting people to join a national socialist pupils' association. We enclose one of these leaflets. A number of pupils have already followed the appeal to join the pupils' association. These considered themselves pledged, in the spirit of the leaflet, to bully those who disagree with them. In the playground these pupils join together and sing national socialist combat songs. Children of republicans are called names, their satchels are smeared with swastikas and they are given leaflets with swastikas or 'Heil Hitler' or 'Germany awake' written on them. In the school in Metjendorf, the son of a republican was beaten up so badly during the break by members of the pupils' association that he had to stay at home for a week.

Source 3: *From* Mein Kampf *by Adolf Hitler, written in 1924 but writing about 1914*

And then came a damp, cold night in Flanders, through which we marched in silence, and when the day began to emerge from the mists suddenly an iron greeting came whizzing at us over our heads, and with a sharp report sent the little pellets flying between our ranks, ripping up the wet ground; but even before the little cloud had passed, from 200 throats the first cheer arose to meet the first messenger of death. Then a crackling and a roaring, a singing and a howling began, and with feverish eyes each one of us was drawn forward, faster and faster, and suddenly past field and hedges the fight began, the fight of man against man. And from the distance the strains of a song reached our ears, coming closer and closer, leaping from company to company, and just as death plunged a busy hand into our ranks the song reached us too and we passed it along: *Deutschland, Deutschland über Alles*. Four days later we came back. Even our step had changed. 17-year-old boys now looked like men.

Source 4: *Cartoon by John Heartfield, drawn in 1924, looking back to 1914. He was on the political left*

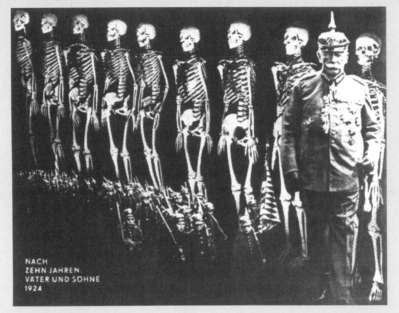

NACH
ZEHN JAHREN:
VÄTER UND SÖHNE
1924

**'After 10 years:
fathers and sons
1924'**

Source 5: *From* Germans into Nazis *by Peter Fritzsche, published in 1998*

National Socialists captured the political imagination of almost one in every two voters because they challenged the authoritarian legacy of the empire, rejected the class-based convictions of social democrats and communists, and both honoured the solidarity and upheld the patriotism of the nation at war. They thus twisted together strands from the political left and the political right, without being loyal to the beliefs of either camp. Mobilising enormous energy and profound expectation for a new beginning, re-imagining the nation as a fiercely nationalistic body politic, and willing to bloody the streets to realise their aims, the Nazis seized power in January 1933 in what amounted to a national revolution.

(a) **Study Source 5**

In what ways does the source indicate that the Nazi Party combined the
ideas of the left and the right? (6 marks)

(b) **Use your own knowledge to explain what the phrase 'children of republicans'
means, as used in Source 2.** (10 marks)

(c) **Study Sources 1 and 2**

To what extent do the two sources agree on the popularity of the Nazi Party
with youth? (10 marks)

(d) **Study Sources 3 and 4**

How useful are these two sources to a historian studying German attitudes
in the 1920s to the First World War? (10 marks)

(e) **Study Sources 2 and 5 and use your own knowledge**

How important was the use of violence by Nazis in their gaining of power
in 1933? (24 marks)

■ ■ ■

Answer to question 2: candidate A

(a) The source indicates that the Nazi Party attacked aspects of political thought
belonging to both the left and right. It challenged the authoritarian views of the
right and rejected the class-based notions of the left. Instead it championed aspects
that could appeal to each, energy and faith in a 'new beginning' for the left and
a strongly nationalistic stance for the right. The two could be combined to form
an overarching structure that appealed to the nation as a whole, aiming to unify
society in much the same way as war was able to.

(b) By 'children of republicans' the writer is referring to children of supporters of the
Weimar Republic, who the Nazi Party came to see as enemies. More specifically,
they included social democrats and Catholics who were considered to be unpatri-
otic and anti-German traditionalism. They were also charged with betraying
Germany in 1919 by signing the Treaty of Versailles, which many on the German
right believed had been unfair and unnecessarily crippling. 'Republicans' was
therefore a catch-all term to describe those supporters of Weimar who were held
to be an obstacle to the establishment of a strong German nation.

(c) Sources 1 and 2 agree in that they obviously both believe that the Nazi Party's
success with the young was worth complaining about. Both see the rising numbers
of young Nazi supporters as a problem. However, the sources differ in terms of the
numbers of children they claim are loyal to the Nazis. Admittedly the writers are
observing different subjects at different times. Source 1 concerns the Protestant
youth movement members in 1931, of whom it claims 70% are Nazi sympathisers.
Source 2 refers more generally to 'schoolchildren' at the slightly earlier date of 1930.
It makes the rather vague assertion that 'a number of pupils' have joined the Nazi
Youth Association. It complains that this group is attacking other children of a non-
Nazi background. It seems to give the impression of a small but forceful minority.

However, according to Source 1, the phenomenon is more widespread (among Protestant children at least). The author writes of a general 'moral' problem, which suggests the movement is more than an unruly minority.

(d) Source 3 is written by Hitler in 1924 about his experiences in the war in 1914. It recalls a personal experience and individual memories and could therefore be biased and unrepresentative of the views of the majority. Hitler also had a very distinctive set of ideas, which he expressed in *Mein Kampf*. He could have invented or exaggerated past events to fit his world view more neatly. In this sense, it pays to be aware of the limitations of the source. Similarly, Source 4, a cartoon, is indicative of the views of one man, the cartoonist, and is, like many cartoons, a little difficult to interpret as the intended message is not always clear. Nevertheless, both sources have their uses. Hitler recalls a determination among the soldiers as they go off to battle, stirred by patriotic feeling induced by the words of *Deutschland, Deutschland über Alles*. The soldiers are thus portrayed as true patriotic heroes. He also recalls the devastating effect of going into battle: '17-year-old boys now looked like men'. Hitler clearly felt these heroes, himself among them, had suffered, but that war, nonetheless, could be glorious. Source 4, however, seems to emphasise the horrors of war above all else. President Hindenburg in the foreground may be a stirring symbol of a patriotic 'father', but the skeletons of the 'sons' who fought in the war loom in the background, pointing to the ultimate futility and waste of war. Thus the two sources are useful indicators of 1920s attitudes to war. Hitler glorifies it more than Heartfield, but also points to the impact this had on those who fought and survived. Heartfield, however, simply emphasises the numbers of young men who pointlessly died.

(e) The Nazis clearly demonstrated that they were willing to use violence, but it was to be just one of the factors in Hitler's rise to power. By the end of March, Hitler was Chancellor and the Nazis, in coalition with the National People's Party in 1933, enjoyed a majority in the Reichstag. This was the result of more than mere brute force.

The SA was responsible for most of the violence committed in the name of the Nazi Party. Indeed it seemed to be their main, if unofficial, function. Violence of this type became noticeably acute during the 1933 election. Communist Party meetings and Social Democrat Party rallies were broken up, and violent street fights erupted. Even the more moderate Catholic Centre Party had its meetings disrupted. Many communists had already been attacked or arrested in the wake of the Reichstag Fire of February 1933. A communist suspect confessed and Hitler used the fire as an excuse to pass a decree 'for the protection of people and state' which gave him emergency powers to place political opponents in custody. This led to 'authorised' violence as opponents were targeted, and demonstrates a clear willingness to use force. Indeed, as Source 2 indicates, this use of force appears to have been part of Nazi culture. Even Nazi youngsters found 'enemies', persecuted and even attacked them. Ultimately, as Source 5 claims, the Nazis were not afraid to 'bloody the streets', and this determination was an important factor in their success.

question

It should be remembered, however, that violence alone did not enable the Nazis to gain power. Germany, in early 1933, was still officially a democracy and Hitler needed to win votes. That he was able to do so impressively (the Nazis gained 43.9% of the vote in the March elections) owed something to the use of force, but also to political skill and popular appeal. As Source 5 claims, the Nazis could appeal effectively to members of both left and right, by combining elements of both and emphasising the nationalistic element of the party, which was to prove a unifying factor. They played to the fears and requirements of particular groups with skill, capitalising, for example, on the middle-class fear of communism. The party was also successful with first-time voters and the young. It was the party of youth and energy, offering hope of a 'new beginning'. Nazi appeal, even to children, is illustrated in Source 2, which shows that in distributing leaflets to playgrounds, and forming the Nazi Youth Association, the Nazis had an effective campaigning machine capable of targeting certain groups. As Source 5 states, they were able to capture almost one in every two voters, an achievement which owed a great deal to clever politics and an effective party machine.

It should be noted that the Nazis made the most of favourable circumstances. The economic slump of 1929–31 led to depression and unemployment, enabling the Nazis to tailor appeals to the disaffected, as they did successfully with peasant farmers, and also to present themselves as a party of order and vitality at a time of disillusionment and chaos. The slump led to the downfall of the coalition government in 1930, creating political uncertainty and setting a precedent for more authoritarian rule. In this climate, Hitler was appointed by President Hindenburg to the position of Chancellor, as he promised the strong leadership the presidential cabinet felt was appropriate for the economic situation. The initial collapse of the democratic coalition government was the fault not only of the economic collapse, but also the result of the system of proportional representation which created unstable coalitions. However, this system was to benefit the Nazis as it allowed them to gain a foothold in the Reichstag and to form a legitimate coalition in 1933, which gave them a majority. In the absence of these circumstances, economic and political, it is doubtful that the Nazi Party would have had such an impact, even with a willingness to resort to violence.

e This is a very good answer. The response to part (a) picks up on all the key points in the text and shows an understanding of the author's argument about the appeal of the NSDAP to both the political right and the political left. It would earn full marks: 6 out of 6.

The response to part (b) is excellent and it would be hard to deny the candidate the full 10 out of 10 marks. It goes beyond simple reference to the Weimar Republic, unpacking the whole concept of republicanism and why the Nazis were so hostile towards it.

Part (c) is answered with clear and effective cross-referencing between the two passages. Similarities and differences are pointed out with appropriate quotations. It would earn full marks: 10 out of 10.

Part (d) is the least effectively answered. Some valid points are made and there is a real attempt to show analysis with pointed reference to the sources. Although the candidate appreciates that the sources represent separate points of view, it is not suggested that they might represent two extreme positions, in between which may lie many alternative responses to war. There is also no exploration of the possible inference that may be drawn from the fact that Source 4 is a cartoon and was therefore published in a journal or magazine. This answer would be awarded 7 out of 10 marks.

The response to part (e) is well structured and focuses clearly on the question asked. The extracts are used well to illustrate both sides of the argument. Points from the extracts are integrated with the student's own knowledge and the whole answer is well written. Perhaps there could have been more on propaganda and the relationship with the old élite, who played such an important part in January 1933. The answer would reach level 4: 20 out of 24 marks.

■ ■ ■

Answer to question 2: candidate B

(a) It is symptomatic of left-wing ideology that the emphasis is placed on the principle in itself almost as a teleologically suspended a priori truth. Thus if it can be said that there is an intimate connection between power and knowledge, in that an increase in knowledge represents a parallel increase in power, then it is not inconceivable that, in light of its sharply defined moral landscape, National Socialism holds an affinity with the left. On the other hand, where the subversive authority in the Nazi Party might be construed as left-wing, the celebration of the Aryan race as superior, and the romanticisation of war and power, all manifest a characteristically right-wing substance of thought. In this respect, as Source 5 demonstrates, National Socialism was, in effect, a 'national revolution'.

(b) The phrase 'children of republicans' has both immediate and more subtle connotations, with regard to the full depth and breadth of its meaning. No doubt it refers, at one level, to those children whose parents were directly involved in the Weimar Republic and, in that respect, pursued a more liberal approach to the dynamics of German politics, favouring a democratisation of power over a centralised and potentially despotic regime. In addition to this, one is struck by an overt sense of indirect loyalty to the republic. That is to say, many children were, in spite of the crude nature of generalisation, the sons and daughters of German citizens simply favouring the retention of the republic and the political dogma and character that defends society from the resentment and distortion of subjectivity.

(c) Source 1 delineates the extent of support for the Nazis amongst the young, yet also expresses some concern as regards the nature of their sympathy for the movement. The report testifies to an approximate 70% of young people supporting National Socialism, explaining this deluge of political fanaticism as without any great epistemological foundation and certainly without the impetus of independent thought. The source records that, contrary to the above, the explanation for National Socialism's overwhelming popularity is to be found in the spirit of the movement and the collective force of the herd. Although one must take into consideration the discontinuity in the dates of the two sources, it is reasonably apparent that little is to impede a conclusion leaning towards a concurrence of evidential verisimilitude. Source 2 indicates the extent of the influence that political theory had over children, yet seems to convey an absence of political direction and more a manipulation of collective judgement and enthusiasm. The mention of bullying, and the almost religious veneration of the swastika and Hitler, betrays a picture of glorified union without the fetters of individual enquiry. Thus it might be said that a conceivable degree of parity exists in the accounts provided by each source, and in that respect, taken together, it might be contended that such was the nature of the youth movement described.

(d) The polarity of these two sources is so incomparably disparate that in themselves they illustrate the diversity of opinion that flourished in the postwar era. Source 3 being, as it is, written by Hitler, is obviously extremely biased, yet serves to illustrate the romanticism of Hitler's nationalism, and his intractable obsession with the drama of war. Whilst there is no explicit desire to conceal the horrors of war, consistent with such a view is the sense of a united nation defying its enemy. Source 4, on the other hand, is clearly designed to accentuate the all-pervading brutality of war and, in a sense, the ineluctable nihilism that accompanies it. This is manifest in the allusion to fathers and sons, which implies that in war, age is of no consequence with regard to the imminence of death. Hence, the two sources are useful as guides to the variance of attitude in the aftermath of the senseless upheaval that comprised the Great War of 1914–18.

(e) Hitler's rise to power was a product of multiple social, economic and political forces, and a process of polarisation began to take place. The Achilles heel of the Weimar Constitution was the political system, which maintained an electoral process based on the intellectual project of modernity and its entailing abstract virtues, such as equality, fairness, democracy and individual rights. The practical application of this affair with idealism was the implementation of proportional representation whereby the constitutive parties laboured under direct accountability to the enfranchised population, which, thus, precluded the possibility of a governmental forum in one party since the immediate correlation between the proportion of the population's vote and the proportion of power hindered the probability of any party achieving a majority. For the smaller, extreme parties, however, this system effectuated shifts of power in their favour, something which is demonstrably the case with the National Socialists. Having increased their number of seats in the Reichstag, their position was consolidated following the run of inept Chancellors, in concurrence with the economic crisis.

It was in this period of prosperity for the Nazis that Hitler excelled in political dexterity. The presentation of the party as a unified and disciplined authority with an inspired and inspiring leader served to propitiate the furtherance of their cause.

In many ways the party was perceived as modern and technologically advanced, with a vision of the future that incited confidence in the disconcerted majority. It is in this respect that the role of violence also played a decisive part in its eventual dominance over the echelons of politics and society. In particular the SA, which formed the paramilitary wing of the party, was used to coerce National Socialist principles throughout the nation, and also to beat up enemies of the National Socialist agenda. Furthermore, as Source 2 indicates, it played a part in encouraging conformity to the party, not only at an adult level but in the pedagogic faculties of the German state as well.

In this respect it is possible to aver a case for the predominance of violence as a means to Hitler's political end, in light of its apparent usage. However, if one is to postulate that an event as convoluted as Hitler's rise to power can be explained without detailed examination of the other contributory factors, one is, in so far as historical truth is an objective and static entity, perverting the image and reality of the past. Hence it is expedient that a more arduous and extensive assessment of Hitler's rise to power be taken into consideration and rigorously scrutinised under the light of empirical fact.

e This candidate has clearly swallowed a dictionary. It is important to realise that one of the skills involved in history is communication. While the candidate shows some understanding of the questions asked, there is often a real failure to communicate this understanding clearly and effectively. Never use big words just for the sake of doing so. The opening sentence in response to (d) illustrates this beautifully. It means the sources show two extreme points of view. Some valid points are made in response to part (b) and the answer would gain 6 out of 10 marks. But more effort should have been put into explaining (in clear English) what the Weimar Republic was and less effort devoted to convoluted expression. This whole answer illustrates that over-complex language can reduce the effectiveness of a response. This is true in the last section, which fails to focus on what is being asked or to make effective use of the extracts. The result is a rather poor level 2 answer, that would be worth only 9 marks out of 24.

Question 3

Source 1: *From an open letter of the German Communist Party addressed to the working voters of the NSDAP and the members of the SA, written in 1931*

In many villages members of the NSDAP, under Communist leadership, have prevented working peasants from having their cows seized or their smallholdings auctioned off. What did your leaders say about that? They forbade every self-help measure. They admonished you to remain within the law. You're supposed to starve legally. Social liberation your leaders promised, but they joined together in Harzburg with the leaders of the big trusts and banks, promising them their faithful service. In Harzburg the SA marched in review for the millionaire, Hugenberg, the finance princes and trust lords. In the economic council of the Brüning government, the big capitalists represented in Harzburg gave their advice, along with the Social Democratic Union leaders, on how the wool can be pulled most quickly over the eyes of the working people. And you were expected to help them. For us there is only one way out — socialism.

Source 2: *From a pamphlet,* National Socialism: A Menace, *published in 1932, written by a conservative critic of the NSDAP*

It is certain that National Socialism does not favour monarchy and is definitely republican in belief. The core of its domestic political programme is the same as that of social democracy on economic, social and tax policy, and largely also in agrarian proposals. Hitler is demanding continuation of the socialist policy that contributed to our economic collapse and harmed the workers as well. His excessive agitation against property and capital, and his unscrupulous provocation of people to militancy, threaten to destroy every possibility of reconstruction by arousing instincts of an envy that will not be easily controlled.

Source 3: *A cartoon entitled* Hitler the National Marxist, *1930. The words which go with the cartoon are 'Adolf, Adolf, give me some of my theories back'*

> **Source 4:** *From the programme of the German Workers' Party (later to become the NSDAP) drawn up by Hitler and Drexler and made public in February 1920*
>
> 12 In view of the enormous sacrifices of life and property demanded of a nation by any war, personal enrichment from war must be regarded as a crime against the nation. We demand therefore the ruthless confiscation of all war profits.
> 13 We demand nationalisation of all businesses which have been formed into corporations (trusts).
> 14 We demand profit-sharing in large industrial enterprises.

> **Source 5:** *From* Germans into Nazis *by Peter Fritzsche, published in 1998*
>
> Although Hitler's appointment to the Chancellorship at the end of January 1933 hinged on the closed-door negotiations of conservatives and out and out monarchists such as Paul von Hindenburg, Alfred Hugenberg and especially Franz von Papen, Hitler would never have figured in their calculus had he not been the leader of Germany's largest party. Much as local élites such as landowners, merchants and clergymen worked with and in due course made National Socialists respectable, Nazi success rested on a broader popular uprising that would challenge and undercut the power of conservative notables throughout the 1920s.

(a) Study Source 1
   In what ways does Source 1 argue that the Nazis' leadership had betrayed
   the interests of ordinary party members? (3 marks)
(b) Explain the phrase used in Source 1, 'the Brüning government'. (5 marks)
(c) Study Sources 1 and 2
   In what ways do the two sources differ in their views of the policy of the
   Nazi leadership? (5 marks)
(d) Study Sources 3 and 4
   How useful are these two sources to a historian studying the socialist nature
   of the Nazi Party between 1920 and 1933? (5 marks)
(e) Study Sources 2 and 5 and use your own knowledge
   Did Hitler come to power as a result of secret deals with conservatives
   or as a result of a broad public support? (12 marks)

■ ■ ■

Answer to question 3: candidate A

(a) Source 1 argues that the Nazi leaders have not acted in the interests of ordinary party members. They had, for example, allowed the seizure of peasant property, and declared that to resist this would be to break the law. According to the source,

question 3

this therefore left the peasants to 'starve legally'. They had also betrayed the ordinary workers by joining forces with the leaders of big business, promising to serve them, and having the SA demonstrate their support in a parade. It implies that the interests of business will be served at the expense of the ordinary man. It claims that important capitalists had already tried to 'pull the wool over the eyes' of the working people, and would continue to do so. It claims that only socialism is true to the interests of the ordinary working German.

(b) Brüning was appointed Chancellor after Müller stepped down in March 1930. He remained in the position until 1932, although his party (the Catholic Centre Party) had no majority and he was reliant upon presidential backing and rule by presidential decree. He pursued a series of deflationary policies in an attempt to address the problems of the economic depression. He cut government expenditure to match falling revenue, a policy which in the long run probably served to increase unemployment. He was sacked in 1932, just as it appeared the worst of the economic slump was over.

(c) Both Sources 1 and 2 are similar in that they are disapproving of the policies of the Nazi leadership. However, here the similarity ends. Both disagree with Nazi policy but for different reasons. Source 1 is a criticism from the Communist Party, while Source 2 is the work of a conservative critic. Source 1 effectively criticises the Nazis for being concerned primarily with winning the support of big business. They are portrayed as capitalists at heart, rather than radicals of left-wing sentiment who would effectively serve the cause of the common man. Source 2, however, criticises the Nazis from the opposite perspective. It claims that the Nazi leadership was 'definitely republican in belief', in that it did not favour the monarchy and was in agreement with the economic, social, tax and agrarian policies of the social democrats. Hitler is therefore accused of continuing the socialist policy of the Weimar government. Source 1, however, is effectively criticising Hitler for failing to show socialist inclinations. Source 2 also claims that the Nazi leadership encouraged militant action; Source 1, however, states that they 'admonished you to remain within the law'. Source 1 therefore essentially sees the Nazis as upholding and reinforcing the established order and staus quo, whereas Source 2 perceives them as threatening it.

(d) Source 4 is an extract from the programme of the early Nazi Party, dated 1920. It shows three points on the programme which are all distinctly socialist. It authorises the confiscation of war profits, the nationalisation of businesses that have become corporations and introduces profit-sharing in large enterprises. Ideas of nationalisation and the confiscation and redistribution of wealth are all core aspects of socialist ideology. In this sense, the extract illustrates that the Nazi Party, or German Workers' Party, as it was in 1920, upheld some distinctly socialist and radical views. However, this is an extract from a programme drawn up very early in the life of the party, and it cannot therefore be deduced that such policies held true until 1933. The extract also shows one small part of the programme, which could feasibly, at other junctures, have contained material of a more 'capitalist' nature. Also, it is certainly fair to say that what the Nazi Party wrote down in terms of political theory was not always adhered to in practice, and policy altered frequently. Source 3 dates from 1930 and suggests that Hitler had 'borrowed' several of Marx's key ideas. This implies that 10 years after Source 4 was written, some commentators still perceived a strong socialist influence on Nazi policy. However, this source, a cartoon, should be treated with caution. It illustrates only the opinion of the cartoonist, who could show bias. He could perhaps be a sympathiser of Hitler's conservative opponents, who often perceived Hitler as a dangerous left-wing radical. As a cartoon it also simplifies complex ideas, and perhaps conveys a general impression rather than a concrete reality.

(e) Hitler was appointed Chancellor in 1933 after conservatives in the presidential cabinet had agreed that he should. However, this was only power of sorts. From his position as Chancellor, Hitler continued to consolidate his power, and was able to do so both as a result of his broad public support base and of his shrewd political skill.

Following the failure of both von Papen and von Schleicher in the role of Chancellor, von Papen proposed the appointment of Hitler to the position of Chancellor. President Hindenburg was reluctant but was persuaded that Hitler could be 'boxed in' and effectively controlled. Hitler would be Chancellor, with his party holding only a minority of the seats in a cabinet with a Conservative majority. As Source 2 illustrates, many conservatives had an innate distrust of Hitler and the Nazi Party, fearing them to be too radical and socialist in their leanings. Nevertheless, the conservatives needed a majority, and Hitler and the 196 seats the Nazis carried in the Reichstag were seen as the best option. Thus, Hitler assumed a key position in government as a direct result of 'closed-door negotiations' among conservatives, as Source 5 states.

However, it must be noted that Hitler was considered in the equation precisely because the Nazis held 196 seats and could lay claim to being the largest party in Germany, as Source 5 also makes clear. This is obviously testament to the Nazis' broad public support. The Nazi ability to gain votes was not only influential in securing Hitler's appointment but was crucial in the coming months as he continued to consolidate and expand his power. The efficient Nazi political machine, with its rallies and campaigns, coupled with the party's ability to appeal to both left and right, to disaffected farmers, and very successfully to first-time voters, led to success in the elections of September 1930, when they gained 107 seats. In March 1933 they gained 288 seats, with almost 45% of the vote. The Nazis formed a coalition with the National People's Party (which had 52 seats) and this allowed them to make the leap from being a minority in a conservative government to leading a government of their own. The conservatives had clearly failed to box Hitler in, and he was now able to exercise real power freely.

Broad public support alone, while crucial in many respects, was married with Hitler's own political skill, without which his hold on power could not have been so spectacularly achieved. This had shown itself during the March elections, as

Hitler used the Reichstag Fire as an excuse to pass an emergency decree 'for the protection of people and state' which authorised the detention of political opponents. This proved helpful in the election, as many leading communists were incarcerated and so unable to campaign. Following the election, Hitler then set out to establish a one-party state and effectively achieved this through the Enabling Act, which, in the absence of the communists, was passed by the Reichstag with a huge majority. Hitler was then free to act without the Reichstag or the President, and was no longer answerable to the electorate. This was a considerable expansion of power, one that was consolidated by the death of President Hindenburg in August 1934, upon which Hitler appointed himself Führer, or leader, of Germany. Such power was obviously not achieved as a result of deals with conservatives alone. The conservative invitation to the position of Chancellor was really an important step-up which gave Hitler a foothold from which to achieve real power.

> 🖉 The response to part (a) contains some irrelevance, i.e. the last two sentences. This tends to turn the response into something of a paraphrase, which is not desirable. Level 1 (4 marks) would be the most that could be given.
>
> The response to part (b) is excellent, being both full and concise. It would be given 10 out of 10 marks.
>
> The answer to part (c) is also excellent, with nicely judged cross-referencing. A good example of this comes in the penultimate sentence. The answer would deserve the full 10 marks.
>
> The response to part (d) is good but not perfect. It would get 8 out of 10 marks. As in a previous answer to a question of this type (see page 51), not enough is made of the purpose of the cartoon.
>
> The response to part (e) shows good integration of sources and some focus, but the knowledge on 'broad support' seems somewhat thin, as it does on the details of 'secret deals'. There is too much focus on the election of March 1933 at the expense of the elections of 1932. In general, the essay shifts from the coming to power to the consolidation of power, without any real justification. It would be awarded at level 3: 14 out of 24 marks.
>
> Overall, this candidate would just secure an A grade.

■ ■ ■

Answer to question 3: candidate B

(a) Source 1 is trying to say that the higher people in the party were not interested in the members of the party, but were only interested in their own power. The source is written by a communist defending the working class, and saying how badly treated working-class people in the Nazi Party are. Also because there were so many people who the Nazis tried to appeal to, it meant that Hitler would end up upsetting some people. This was because Hitler was an opportunist, which becomes particularly clear in the 1930s with his foreign policy.

(b) The 'Brüning' government refers to the government under the Chancellor Brüning, who ruled in 1930. He was appointed by Hindenburg the President, to deal with the economic crisis that had been happening since 1929, but he failed because his policy was too deflationary, and didn't help the economy. A part of this deflationary policy was to cut public expenditure, and also increase taxation. Unfortunately this made the whole thing worse and he was sacked by Hindenburg.

(c) Source 5 explains how the leadership of the Nazi Party was important because it was the largest party in the Weimar Republic, and because of that it enabled them to work their way into power. It says that the only reason Hitler was appointed to the Chancellorship was because he was leader of Germany's largest party. Source 1 explains that the reason for the strength of this leadership was because of Hitler's ability to appeal to lots of different groups in the country, which gave him the financial support he needed to expand the party, and also meant that he didn't alienate any groups (except Marxists, Jews and gypsies). Source 5 also says how Hitler's appointment depended on the failure of the conservatives at the time of financial disaster. It is important to understand the *Führerprinzip* or Führer principle which stresses the importance of the leader of the party as a guiding force for the nation. So Hitler, through National Socialism, would hold influence over lots of different people in society.

(d) Source 3 is a cartoon showing Marx and Hitler. The cartoon is hoping to show that some of Hitler's ideas were taken from Marx. That is why the caption says 'Adolf, Adolf, give me some of my theories back'. Source 4 gives a section of the programme from the German Workers' Party from 1920. The three points of the programme are socialist in their ideas. Point 12 demands that no profits are to be made out of war, and so the state should confiscate all the profits, because that is fairer. Point 13 says that the German Workers' Party wanted to nationalise all businesses, which is a socialist policy. Also point 14 states how the Nazis hope to redistribute the money they have made from their confiscations and nationalisation. So the reason Marx is asking Adolf for his theories back in Source 3 is because there was a part of Hitler's ideas that was concerned with the moral authority of the state over the choice of individuals, which is Marxist. So there are good reasons for saying that Hitler took some ideas from Marx, even though Hilter claimed to despise both Marx and Marxists. This makes it all very interesting for the historian, especially Source 4 since it is a product of Nazi thought, and so would not deliberately claim to have anything in common with Marx. Because of this the sources give an interesting portrayal of Nazi ideas, since the Nazis are usually seen to be a right-wing party.

(e) You can say that Hitler came to power because he was very good at making deals with conservatives, but you can't ignore the fact that he had a lot of support as well.

In Hitler's early days his attempt at power had been badly organised and the Munich Putsch of 1923 ended in disaster, which he learned from when he was put in prison afterwards. In this period he wrote *Mein Kampf* which is the bedrock of Nazi ideology, and after this he reorganised the party more effectively. The appeal

of the Nazis at the end of the 1920s and in the early 1930s is due to a whole series of factors. They were more popular in Protestant areas of Germany than amongst the Catholics, which is why they never had any big effect on the Centre Party, which was Catholic. They were particularly popular in rural areas and amongst farmers, landowners and the lower classes of rural society as well. This was partly because of the idea of the folk community which they made a lot of use of, attracting those in small rural communities. Although at first the Nazis found it hard to attract people from urban areas, by 1932 they had found support amongst the upper middle class and the richer suburban areas, appealing to the well-paid middle class, like teachers and doctors. Hitler also managed to win over support from big business, which provided financial support for his campaigning, and gained him more respectability amongst politicians. But there were many other factors in the personal strength of the Nazis. At one level they had a modern image, and were mainly made up of young men, standing in contrast to the older politicians of the time. There was also a general fear of communism at a time when politics was in chaos, so many felt that they had no alternative. Not only that, but Hitler was a very good speaker who aroused emotional support. The SA and the SS were important for their discipline when things were bad, and also for their ability to force support onto the public.

Hitler's relationship with conservative politics was important and must not be passed by casually. When the Great Coalition government in 1930 collapsed, Hitler's links with the nationalists paid off. What followed was a lot of chancellors who were unable to solve the economic problems which ultimately forced Hindenburg to appoint Hitler as Chancellor, since the right-wing believed that he wouldn't last very long and could be replaced without too much trouble. Not only that, they didn't see any great threat in the man. The initial figure was Heinrich Brüning, a member of the Centre Party who tried to solve the economic problems by cutting expenditure and increasing taxes. He was followed by von Papen, another member of the Centre Party, but he was got rid of because he didn't have enough support in the Reichstag. He was followed by General von Schleicher, but he failed to group together a coalition. Hitler was then invited to form a government by Hindenburg. Because Hitler had the support of the army and big business, he was in a suitable position to be chosen to form a right-wing authoritarian government.

In spite of the relation with conservatives and the role of popularity in Hitler becoming Chancellor, it is also important to understand that there were problems with the system that made him become Chancellor. The Weimar Republic ran on a system of proportional representation, which meant that governments were coalitions, since no one could form a majority. This meant that the extreme parties, if people voted for them, would be represented in the Reichstag. Also article 48 of the constitution undermined democracy and many people resented such a quick change, including the army, the civil service and the judiciary. The economic recovery of the middle part of the 1920s was important too in the rise to power of Hitler. The Dawes Plan, which was money taken from America as a loan, was invested in the wrong way, and the country over-relied on loans from America which made it worse when the Wall Street crash happened in 1929, and America asked for the loans back. The crisis was also an important factor because it was the middle class, the young, the farmers and apprentices that initially suffered and it was to them that Hitler appealed.

So it is clear that both Hitler's relationship with the conservatives and his popularity were important. But it is also important to see that the way the Republic treated Germany's economic recovery, and the fact of the economic depression, were decisive in the rise to power of Hitler.

e The response to part (a) is not good as it contains many irrelevant details. At best it would deserve 2 out of 6 marks.

The response to part (b) is better and would be awarded level 2 (6 marks). There is much accurate and valid information but nothing about Brüning's lack of a majority or his need to rely on presidential decrees.

The response to part (c) is an illustration of the classic mistake for these comparative questions, i.e. comparing the wrong extracts. It would not earn any marks.

The answer to (d) at least looks at the right two extracts but it ignores many obvious and relevant points. No attention is paid to the dating of the two documents or their purpose. It would merit only 4 out of 10 marks.

Although the response to part (e) sometimes wanders away from the main point, there is in general an attempt to define 'broad support', although there appears to be very thin knowledge about 'secret deals'. The main weakness is a failure to make explicit use of the extracts and therefore the highest mark possible would be level 2 (8 marks).

Overall, this would barely merit a pass.

Question 4

Source 1: *From* Germany's Hitler *written by Heinz A. Heinz and published in 1934 but written in about 1921*

I stuck myself in a corner and kept my eyes and ears well open. The first thing I seemed to notice was that this wasn't a mere bourgeois gathering and no highbrow one either. The audience was made up of plain folk like myself, working men and petty shopkeepers. Then this man Hitler got up to speak. I saw at once this was no common or garden tubthumper, no gas bag like most of them. Everything he said was just common sense and sound. Although I wasn't one to be won over all in a moment, it didn't take me no longer than the first meeting to realise that Hitler was straight as a die and a safe one to put your shirt on. I went to every one of his meetings after that. Bit by bit he won me round. He got in blow after blow at all the ideas I had been holding onto up to now and laid them out flat! He knocked the red nonsense out of me — all about the world revolution to put the world right — hot-air like that. Instead I seemed to see what he was driving at. Instead of prophecies, far-off Utopias and the like, in National Socialism he gave us a good working scheme of things we could be busy on right away.

Source 2: *From* Darkness over Germany *by E. Buller, published in 1941 but telling the story of a young German in 1931*

At the end of my time in university, I was unemployed for a year so I went back to do some research work in the hope that perhaps times would improve. But for five years I remained unemployed and I was broken in body and spirit and I learnt how stupid all my dreams were in those hard days at the university. I was not wanted by Germany, and certainly if I was not wanted here I was not wanted anywhere in the world... Just then I was introduced to Hitler. You don't understand and I cannot explain either because I don't know what happened. But life for me took on a tremendous new significance. After all, Germany would rise again; after all, I was wanted. I've since committed myself, body soul and spirit to this movement for the resurrection of Germany.

Source 3: *From* Germans into Nazis *by Peter Fritzsche, published in 1998*

To regard, as so many observers still do, the Nazis as conservatives or reactionaries or the petit bourgeois shock troops of big capital is to miss the destruction they wrought on the traditional parties and the violent politics they made acceptable. Their aggressive nationalism and virulent anti-Semitism and their élitist conception of leadership did not erase their populist and anti-capitalist appeal.

Source 4: *Elections to the Reichstag (% vote)*

Elections	Political parties (% of vote)						
	NSDAP	DNVP	DVP	Centre	DDP	SPD	KPD
May 1924	6.5	19.5	9.5	16.6	5.7	21.6	12.6
December 1924	3.0	20.5	10.1	17.3	6.3	26.0	9.0
May 1928	2.6	14.2	8.7	15.2	4.8	29.8	10.6
September 1930	18.3	7.0	4.9	14.8	3.5	24.5	13.1
July 1932	37.3	5.9	1.2	15.7	1.0	21.6	14.3
November 1932	33.1	8.5	1.8	15.0	1.0	20.4	16.9

(a) Study Source 1

   Why did the author react so positively to Hitler? (6 marks)

(b) Explain what is meant by the phrases 'élitist conception of leadership' and
   'anti-Semitism', used in Source 3. (10 marks)

(c) Study Sources 3 and 4

   How far does Source 4 support the statements made in Source 3 about
   the effects of the rise of the NSDAP on traditional parties? (10 marks)

(d) Study Sources 1 and 2

   How valuable are these sources in explaining Hitler's widespread appeal? (10 marks)

(e) Study Sources 3 and 4 and use your own knowledge

   Explain the growing popularity of the NSDAP between 1929 and the
   end of 1932. (24 marks)

■ ■ ■

Answer to question 4: candidate A

(a) The author, Heinz A. Heinz, was well disposed towards Hitler from the moment
he surveyed the audience. He felt it was made up of 'plain folk like myself, working
men and petty shopkeepers'. When Hitler spoke, Heinz felt he spoke 'common
sense', was honest and straightforward ('straight as a die') and a man who could
safely be entrusted with responsibility. He also felt that in National Socialism, Hitler
had presented a 'good working scheme' with real, tangible measures, not merely
abstract ideas.

(b) Nazi ideology was inherently élitist. It regarded the Aryan race as superior, while
certain races, such as the Jews, were inferior, even parasitic, and should be kept
away from positions of power. This hostility to Jews is what the author means by
anti-Semitism, which was to manifest itself throughout the Nazi era, from the early
attacks upon Jewish property to the full horrors of the Holocaust. Anti-Semitism
is closely related to the Nazi 'élitist conception of leadership'. They regarded

leadership as something you were naturally born for, not something that could be obtained by anyone through merit, as a democratic system theoretically encourages. Only a limited few were born to lead, typically those who showed all the 'finest' qualities of the Aryan race, as exemplified by the SS.

(c) The author of Source 3 writes of the 'destruction' that the Nazis 'wrought on the traditional parties'. Source 4 shows this to be true in many respects. It gives the percentage of the vote obtained by each of the major parties from May 1924 to November 1932. The NSDAP shows a remarkable rise in popularity from a low of 2.6% in May 1928 to 33.1% in November 1932. This increase in votes does indeed appear to have come at the expense of four of the major parties. The DNVP's vote fell from 14.2% in May 1928 to 5.9% in July 1932 (it did, however, rise a little in November). The DVP's share fell from 8.7% in May 1928 to 1.8% by 1932 while the DDP showed a similar pattern as their share of the vote also dropped from 4.8% to 1% by November 1932. The SPD's, or Socialist Party's, percentage of the vote also fell considerably, but they were still left with 20.4% of the vote in November 1932, the second largest party in the Reichstag. The Centre Party appears to have been relatively unaffected by the rise of the Nazis. Its share of the vote managed to remain constant, around the 15% mark, although dipping slightly in 1930 to 14.8%. The statement made in Source 3 cannot therefore be applied to the Centre Party. Nor is it true of the KPD, or Communist Party, whose share of the vote actually increased from 10.6% in 1928 to 16.9% in November 1932. One suspects, therefore, that while many parties were losing votes to the Nazis, votes were also being lost to the Communists. Indeed, this could perhaps explain the fall in SPD support, as left-wing voters turned to the more radical policies of the KPD. Source 3 is also a little unjustified in writing of the 'destruction' of the traditional parties. Admittedly support for the DDP and the DVP was reduced to less than 2%, but the Centre Party, SPD and the KPD retained a healthy presence. The NSDAP, however, by November 1932 had obtained unquestioned dominance, a fact which would give the impression that rival parties had been quashed.

(d) Both Sources 1 and 2 are published (and, one assumes, written) at least 10 years after the events they describe. They could both, therefore, contain inaccuracies due to failing memory or manifest a desire to restructure the past to fit more neatly with the present. They are also both accounts of individual experience and therefore carry all the potential pitfalls of sources of this kind. They could contain bias and must not be assumed to be typical. Generalisations can only be drawn with caution, as it is not inevitable that all men of similar backgrounds would have chosen to be Nazis. Indeed, they could just as easily have become communists, as the author of Source 1 had done for a while. Nevertheless, they do illuminate important aspects of Nazi appeal. The author of Source 1 regards himself as one of society's 'plain folk'. He was attracted by Hitler's simple, direct 'common sense' approach and regarded him as honest and 'safe', bringing practical solutions ('a good working scheme') with real policies that ordinary people could understand. The author contrasts this favourably with the 'far-off Utopias' promised by communism. Source 2 also suggests that Hitler's appeal lay largely in the solutions he offered, and gives the impression of the Nazi Party as a haven for the dis-affected. Hitler offered 'new hope' to a man 'broken in body and spirit' by 5 years of unemployment. Hitler promised a new, revitalised Germany, which not only offered an end to economic hardship, but also encouraged a more abstract patri-otic notion. The idea that Germany could be 'resurrected' and restored to her former glory was a prospect that could attract support across the political spectrum. The two sources, and Source 1 in particular, also point to another aspect of universal Nazi appeal — Hitler's personal charisma. He clearly had tremendous ability as an orator, and was able not only to hold an audience but to convince them to alter their opinions. Both authors write of the time they encountered Hitler as a turning point in their lives. Admittedly this could be over-dramatised for the purpose of making the publications more interesting and should therefore be treated with some caution. Nevertheless, the statistics show that the Nazis did obtain a higher percentage of votes than their rivals, and these sources can shed a little light on why this was the case.

(e) The election statistics show a remarkable rise in the popularity of the NSDAP. As Source 4 indicates, their share of the vote rose from 2.6% in May 1928 to 33.1% in November 1932. This impressive turn-around was the result of several factors.

The Nazi Party demonstrated many unique strengths which contributed directly to their success. Their policies and political style enabled them to lure many voters away from the traditional parties. Source 3 emphasises this point and is supported by the evidence in Source 4, which shows a decline in the number of votes obtained by the DNVP, DVP, DDP and the SPD. With the possible exception of the SPD, which may have lost more votes to the KPD that it did to the Nazis, these other parties were losing a high proportion of their largely middle-class vote. The Nazis must therefore have been offering something the other parties were not. As far as the middle classes were concerned, the Nazi stance on law and order, with its highly disciplined SA parades and public condemnation of communists, made them appealing as a 'safe' option to restore order to a country that had experienced great upheaval in the aftermath of the First World War, the collapse of the Weimar Republic and the economic slump. They also offered not only the restoration of order but of Germany's former greatness. The highly nationalist theme that ran through all Nazi policy, often aggressively so, as Source 3 indicates, appealed across all sections of society. This was particularly true of those, usually conservative in sentiment, who felt that Germany had been cheated and betrayed by those who had signed the Treaty of Versailles in 1919. They felt that the country needed to return to the glory of the prewar era, before the dark days of 'republicanism'.

The Nazis were also a young, dynamic and energetic party, who promised to get things done, and in this way were able to appeal to the less conservative elements in society. The Weimar Republic had been plagued by unstable, ineffectual coalitions, and the vigour and unity of the Nazis contrasted favourably with that. They offered a clear programme of ideas that provided ready solutions.

They were also new, untried and untainted by failure, which endeared them to those who had grown frustrated with the old regime. The Nazis furthered this appeal with a fresh style of campaigning. The use of parades, rallies and widely distributed propaganda effectively conveyed the Nazi message. This was wedded to Hitler's own personal charisma and fantastic ability as a speaker. His speeches were real pieces of showmanship and showed a fervour rarely seen in parliamentary politics.

However, it is important to remember that whatever the positive strengths of the NSDAP, it was helped enormously by circumstances. The Wall Street Crash of 1929 triggered an economic slump in Germany which was to have significant repercussions. Unemployment increased dramatically, leading to poverty and disillusionment, often among the young, who saw the Nazis as offering hope for the future and an outlet for their frustrations. Small business owners were also hard hit, and responded well to the Nazi promise of economic recovery. Peasant farmers, too, suffered under a severe agricultural depression, and became the target of a Nazi campaign in the countryside which was to prove extremely fruitful. Rural farmers, after all, comprised almost 30% of voters. Economic hardship and unemployment had the effect of increasing communist support, which in turn frightened the middle classes. The depression had also led to political disarray as the coalition government collapsed in 1930 and was replaced by a more authoritarian government, headed by the presidential cabinet. Germany therefore appeared to be both economically and politically unstable. In such a climate of economic hardship, disillusionment and uncertainty, Nazi energy and the promise to restore Germany to its former glory held particularly potent appeal.

e The response to part (a) shows a real comprehension of the arguments advanced by the author of Source 1. It makes the obvious inference that the author is a working-class person. It would be rewarded 6 out of 6 marks.

The response to part (b) clearly tackles both phrases but there is an error of understanding in the reference to merit, a concept of which the Nazis approved. This would gain 8 marks.

The response to part (c) is excellent and would deserve full marks. There is clear cross-referencing and good analysis of Source 4.

The response to part (d) is good, although possibly the point about the social range of the two sources (i.e. the author of Source 1 is a working man, by implication, and the author of Source 2 is a graduate) needs making. Eight out of 10 marks would be appropriate here.

Part (e) is well answered, with excellent use made of Source 4. Source 3 is not as well used. It would be worth 18 marks out of 24.

Overall, this would be an A-grade answer.

■ ■ ■

Answer to question 4: candidate B

(a) The reason Heinz A. Heinz reacts so positively in Source 1 is because of the nature of Hitler's speech. In the early part of the 1920s, politics was dominated by a profusion of different political ambitions. Most of these were largely dogmatically driven, and concerned with idealistic paradigmatic visions of the future. Those, on the other hand, who were attracted by Hitler wanted something more practical and mundane, which would actually improve the nature of their contemporary socio-economic climate. What someone like the author wanted was a series of practical solutions to a series of practical problems, without the circumlocutions of other politicians.

(b) By 'élitist conception of leadership' Source 3 means the *Führerprinzip* or leader principle of Nazi ideology. This refers to the importance of a strong leader to represent the collective will of the nation, and to carry the nation forward. It meant that total power was invested in Hitler, and he could use it to do anything he liked without being accountable to anyone. 'Anti-Semitism' is hostility and prejudice towards Jews and was something adopted by Hitler. It concerns Hitler's abhorrence of the Jewish race as inferior, manipulative, selfish, ugly and in every way parasites. Hitler used the Jews as a scapegoat for all the problems that Germany faced, especially following the economic crisis of 1929. Anti-Semitism was to culminate in the 'Final Solution' and the Holocaust which was an attempt to 'liberate' the German race from the influence of Jewry, thus demonstrating how stupid Hitler was.

(c) Source 4 is a table of the changing percentage of the vote the different parties received between May 1924 and November 1932. It shows how the Nazis started off as a minority party in 1924 with 6.5% of the vote, and went into decline during the period from 1924 to 1929. Yet it clearly illustrates a significant increase from 1930 to 1932. Looking at the other parties it is possible to discern decline amongst the parties of the conventional right and left, with the Catholic Centre remaining fairly consistent. This suggests that Hitler managed to appeal to those sectors of society favouring a market-driven economy. The decline in support for the conventional left might suggest a case for arguing that they also managed to appeal to those who believed in the importance of the state as a moral regulator. Source 3 largely agrees with this in that it says that despite arguments for the Nazis being at both ends of the political spectrum, they managed to appeal to everyone.

(d) Source 1 recounts the experience of Heinz A. Heinz looking back on his first encounters with the German Workers' Party in 1921. He explains how the party was not as intellectually motivated as other parties, and there was a more down to earth feel of honesty and normality about it. Hearing Hitler speak, he recalls that everything he said was common sense, rather than abstruse theorising. He also explains how it was only gradually that he came around to Hitler's point of view, having been seduced by the allure of Hitler's character and policies. Source 2 describes the story of a young German in 1931. He tells of how, prior to

Hitler's ascension to power, he felt greatly disenchanted with himself in relation to his social milieu and his nation. Yet, when Hitler arrived on the scene, he describes the sense of purpose and direction his life acquired, and equally how he felt reunited with his nation.

(e) Whereas the growing popularity of the NSDAP between 1929 and the end of 1932 might be explained through cursory reference to all manner of factors, it is necessary to take into consideration the fact that some were of greater importance than others.

Source 4, in itself, provides useful information. At first glance it shows that the Nazis attracted a monumental increase in the percentage of the votes between 1930 and 1932. What is interesting, however, is the way in which the other parties change. The conservative parties (the DNVP and the DVP) both decline radically in the latter period as does the socialist party (DDP). This would suggest that during this period the votes that would usually have gone to these parties went to the more extreme parties, since precisely at this point both the extreme right-wing (the NSDAP) and the extreme left-wing (KPD) increase in their percentage of the vote. It was at this time that economic problems were raging throughout the country. Hence it is understandable that people would begin to look for parties offering alternative solutions to the prevailing problems.

Source 3 offers a further reason for the increase in popularity of the NSDAP between 1929 and the end of 1932. The author argues that it is inaccurate to maintain that the Nazis had a greater affinity with either the conservatives or the socialists, since an aspect of their political agenda was to appeal to as many disparate groups as possible. This, he argues, is evident by virtue of the fact that people have attempted to make a case for a more reactionary character in their politics and, conversely, a conservative one as well. As he points out, their concern with the *Führerprinzip*, which is essentially top-down in its nature, their nationalism and their anti-Semitism didn't prevent them from appealing to other groups. For this reason it could be argued that a part of Hitler's success was his ability to appeal to a diversity of groups. Because the political system was one of proportional representation, this inevitably improved Hitler's chances of political success.

In this way, as Sources 3 and 4 explain, the growing popularity of the NSDAP between 1929 and 1932 can be explained both by the decline of the conventional left and right at a time of crisis, and by the Nazis' vast appeal.

The response to part (a) contains genuine comprehension, despite some rather ornate language. The clear inference that the author is working class is missed, so the candidate would be awarded at level 1 (4 marks).

The response to part (b) contains much valid information, although the broader implications of the élitist view of leadership are not fully explained. Nevertheless, 8 marks would be earned here.

The answer to part (c) contains much valid analysis of Source 4, but direct cross-reference, as demonstrated in candidate A's answer (page 66), is weaker than one might have hoped for. This answer would deserve level 2 (6 marks).

The response to part (d) is an excellent example of what not to do. The candidate merely summarises the two extracts and avoids the central thrust of the question. It would be given 3 marks out of 10 at the most.

The answer to part (e) shows some genuine understanding, but it is short and relies heavily on the two extracts rather than the candidate's own knowledge. It would be awarded at level 2: 10 marks out of 24.

This candidate would probably be capable of getting an A grade but, because of silly mistakes, would end up with a C.

Question 5

Source 1: *From the evidence given by Franz von Papen at his trial in Nuremberg. This was published in 1946 but refers to the events of 1933*

Further support of the von Schleicher presidential cabinet by means of a declaration of a state of emergency and the suspension of Parliament, which was against the constitution, had been rejected by the Reich President on the 23rd. He rejected these proposals — as we know, von Schleicher had told him in December that a violation of the constitution would mean civil war and a civil war would mean chaos — because he said I am not in a position with the army and with the police to maintain law and order. Since Hitler offered to participate in a presidential cabinet, this was the only remaining possibility and all the forces and political parties which supported my government in 1932 were available for this.

Q. What were the instructions which the Reich President gave you?

A. The instructions given me by von Hindenburg were as follows: the formation of a government under the leadership of Hitler, with the utmost restriction of National Socialist influence and within the framework of the constitution.

Source 2: *From a letter from the British Ambassador in Germany to the British Foreign Secretary in March 1933*

The new press decree of the 6 February goes far beyond anything which has yet appeared in this country. It gives the government power to suppress a newspaper once and for all, for suppression for the space of a year means economic ruin nowadays. By suppressing newspapers, proclaiming meetings, arresting speakers and monopolising the wireless, the government can render the task of their opponents difficult.

Source 3: *From* The Nazi Seizure of Power *by William Sheridan Allen, a study of a single German town during the 1930s, published in 1965*

In the week-long campaign before the local elections, Northeim's SPD was not allowed to hold meetings or to pass out campaign literature. They did manage to place one advertisement in the town paper but, doubtless because of their previous experience of being refused advertising space, the SPD made that a very cautious, almost perfunctory notice, in language that contrasts so sharply with previous socialist advertisements that the publication probably did the SPD more harm than good:

'To the voters of Northeim! On Sunday, March 12th, important elections will be held, namely for the provincial diet, County Council and City Council. The SPD has presented its own list for all these elections which bears the number '2'. We call upon the populace to vote early and vote in each case for the list number '2'.

Source 4: *Election results in March 1933 for the city of Northeim and its surrounding area, given in* The Nazi Seizure of Power *by William Sheridan Allen, published in 1965*

Political party	City Council election March 1933 (number of votes)	County Council election March 1933 (number of votes)
NSDAP	4,565(a)	4,273
DNVP	(a)	456
DVP	(a)	0
SPD	1,677	1,650
Centre	0	0
KPD	43	0

Note (a): The NSDAP, DNVP and DVP fought the City Council election as the National Unity Coalition.

Source 5: *From* The Third Reich *edited by Christian Leitz, published in 1999*

Even before he was sworn into office, Hitler outplayed for the first time the two potentially most powerful cabinet members, Vice-chancellor von Papen and the economic dictator, the Minister of Economics and Agriculture, Hugenberg. He convinced them to agree to the dissolution of the Reichstag followed by new elections, a process which could only benefit the NSDAP. During the period of election campaigning which ended on the 5th March, the government parties received substantial financial support from big business even though (with the exception of a pro-Hitler wing already active in 1932) a majority had previously given preference to a government led by von Papen to one led by Hitler.

(a) Study Source 1

   Why, according to von Papen, did Hindenburg agree to appoint Hitler Chancellor? (6 marks)

(b) Explain the phrase 'within the framework of the constitution' as used in Source 1. (10 marks)

(c) Study Sources 2 and 3

   How far does Source 3 support the opinions expressed in Source 2? (10 marks)

(d) Study Sources 3 and 4

How valuable are the figures given in Source 4 in the light of the information given in Source 3 to a historian wishing to assess the extent of Nazi support in Germany in March 1933? (10 marks)

(e) Study Sources 3 and 5 and use your own knowledge

Explain how the Nazis consolidated their power between January and the end of March 1933. (24 marks)

■ ■ ■

Answer to question 5: candidate A

(a) According to von Papen, Hindenburg agreed to appoint Hitler fundamentally because he was 'the only remaining possibility'. He appears to have shared von Schleicher's fear that to continue ruling indefinitely by Presidential Decree (and thus violating the constitution) would result in chaos and even civil war. It was felt that the army and the police could not be relied upon to keep order. Therefore, as Hitler carried a great deal of support and possessed a formidable presence in the Reichstag, which could not be ignored, he was the obvious choice to appoint to the position of Chancellor. Hindenburg seems to have regarded this as a prefer- able alternative to civil disorder and believed that a government under Hitler's leadership, which upheld the constitution, and which could be sufficiently controlled so as to ensure the 'utmost restriction of National Socialist influence', was the best option available.

(b) When von Papen uses the phrase 'within the framework of the constitution' he is referring to the Weimar Constitution as created in 1919. This framework for government posed many problems, notably the system of proportional repre- sentation it introduced which created a multiplicity of parties and necessitated coalition government. These governments were therefore prone to disagreement and fracture, leading to instability and constant fluctuation. The constitution had many critics, not only as a result of the flaws it contained but also by its very existence. Many on the right, for example, felt the Weimar government marked a betrayal of tradition, and wished to restore the monarchy and Germany's prewar system of government. Many on the left, in contrast, felt that the constitution did not go far enough in its efforts to encourage equality and democracy. However, from the collapse of the coalition government in 1930 to the appointment of Hitler to the position of Chancellor in 1933, the constitution had effectively been ignored. Hindenburg and the presidential cabinet had been ruling by decree. Ironically, it was hoped that the appointment of Hitler would mark a return to parliamentary government, which would once again operate 'within the framework of the constitution'.

(c) Source 2 is written by a British observer of the effects of the press decrees of February 1933. It claims that the government has the power to destroy newspapers by suppressing them for a year, which he feels would inevitably lead to 'economic ruin'. This is used against the publications of opponents, who are then further intimidated in other ways, as their meetings are disrupted and members arrested, making any form of opposition difficult. Source 3 gives an account of an election campaign in Northeim. It supports Source 2 in that it records the suppression of the SPD. They were forbidden, for example, to hold meetings or distribute campaign literature. They did manage to obtain one advertising space, however, suggesting that with determination, the press could be utilised by Nazi opponents. Nevertheless, the advert that appears gives no indication of the socialist manifesto, makes no attack on the opposition and is merely a very toned down, almost deliberately abstruse request to vote for the SPD. This suggests that Nazi control of the town paper was actually fairly tight. Indeed, the advertisement appears almost as a token, published to make the election look at least marginally democratic. The evidence in Source 3 does therefore support the assertion made in Source 2 that the Nazi government was able to 'render the task of their opponents difficult' by successfully limiting their activities.

(d) At first glance the figures given in Source 4 show an impressive victory for the NSDAP coalition in Northeim for the elections of March 1933. It could therefore be concluded that support for the Nazis was overwhelming in this area, an assumption which could be important for the historian wishing to analyse the Nazi support base. However, the evidence given in Source 3 rather undermines the overwhelming Nazi victory. Opposing parties were clearly unable to operate and so establish a true contest. As the Centre Party received no votes at all, it seems reasonable to assume that they did not compete, or were prevented from doing so. Source 3 states that the SPD were forbidden to hold meetings or distribute literature. They were allowed only one 'perfunctory' advertisement in the town paper. As such, it cannot have been an equal opponent. Many voters may have felt that there was no contest, the only option was to vote for the NSDAP. The true extent of opposition support may therefore be misrepresented. If the historian was wishing to draw conclusions about Nazi support across Germany as a whole, he would have to be wary of generalising from the results of one town, or even one county. Levels of support varied from area to area. It must also be noted that the result given for the City Council of Northeim shows the collective result for the coalition of the NSDAP, the DNVP and the DVP, and does not give a party breakdown. We cannot therefore be certain of how many of the 4,565 votes cast came specifically from Nazi supporters, although the County Council votes suggest that most did.

(e) Hitler was appointed Chancellor on 30 January 1933 and therefore seemed to have obtained power. In reality he was very dependent on the DNVP and the goodwill of the President. However, over the next 3 months he proceeded to consolidate and expand his influence and the hold of the Nazi Party and had considerable success in only a short time. Thus, by the end of March 1933, his position was much stronger.

As Source 5 indicates, one of Hitler's first moves was to call for the dissolution of the Reichstag and a new election in March. He was able to persuade powerful cabinet members, von Papen and Hugenberg among them, to agree to this, proving that his influence in the presidential cabinet could not be suppressed. The aim was obviously to increase the number of Nazi seats in the Reichstag and so ensure Hitler, as the head of a government, had a Nazi majority with which he could alter the constitution. His plan worked eventually, but the Nazis did not do as well as they expected. The election returns gave the NSDAP 43.9% of the vote and 288 seats in the Reichstag. Hitler could then form a government with a majority with only the support of the DNVP, who would form a small minority in a government with an overwhelming Nazi majority.

This electoral success was a result of shrewd political manoeuvring on Hitler's part. In February the Reichstag building caught fire and burned down. A communist suspect was arrested and confessed to arson. While it appears that he was in fact acting independently, Hitler used the fire as an excuse to crack down on the opposition, the communists in particular. On 28 February he issued a decree for 'the protection of the people and state', which gave the government special powers to suspend all civil liberties and place opponents in custody. Many leading communists were therefore incarcerated and so prevented from campaigning in the forthcoming elections. Although this decree was declared a temporary measure, it was never withdrawn, and therefore legalised the arrest and intimidation of opponents. This act was reinforced by the press decrees, also passed in February, which effectively gave the Nazis control of the press, which would be extremely detrimental to their opponents. Source 3 illustrates this control of opposition in its account of the suppression of the SPD in Northeim. The SPD had its activities severely restricted. It was forbidden to hold meetings and distribute publicity, and was prevented from using the local press as a platform. Opposition was therefore kept to a minimum. The SA played a crucial role in this process and manifested the Nazi willingness to use force for political gain. They were on hand to disperse the meetings of political opponents and engage in physical intimidation, whether openly fighting with communists in the streets or making their presence felt on the doors of polling stations. They also served a more positive role by forming the backbone of the Nazi parades, which presented an impressive spectacle of order and discipline and were to appeal strongly to many voters. Thus the Nazis forced themselves onto centre stage and into a position in which society was forced to take note of them.

As Source 5 points out, Hitler also made a concerted effort to gain the support of big business. Until 1933, with the exception of a minority, most business leaders had refrained from throwing their weight behind Hitler. However, his efforts were successful and the Nazis gained not only the political weight that such support entailed but important financial aid. With the support of the country's financial élite and, in the wake of the election, apparently a large proportion of the populace, Hitler had effectively consolidated his power and was in a position to exercise it freely. All that remained was to alter the constitution. To do this, Hitler needed a two-thirds majority. He achieved this as a result of a deal with the Centre Party.

The result was the passing of the Enabling Bill. This conferred upon Hitler dictatorial powers. The Weimar Republic had effectively committed suicide.

℮ The response to part (a) would get the full 6 marks. Not only does it explain the stated reasons for Hitler's appointment but it also picks up on the important inference at the end that the President believed that Hitler could be controlled and Nazi influence limited.

The response to part (b) would also deserve full marks, showing an understanding of the Weimar Constitution and the particular situation of 1933.

The response to part (c) is good and would be worth 8 out of 10 marks. There is an excellent understanding of the two sources and a nice awareness at the end that the word 'difficult', rather than 'impossible', has been used in Source 2. For full marks there should have been more integration of the two sources rather than simply dealing with Source 2 and then Source 3.

The response to part (d) picks up on most of the key points, analysing Source 4 in the light of the information given in Source 3. As with so many candidates' answers on the value of sources to a historian, the negative side is given more weight than the positive. The answer would be worth 8 marks out of 10.

The response to part (e) makes good use of the sources by integrating information from them into the text, but the answer seems somewhat thin and could certainly do with a concluding paragraph. This would be a level 3 response, earning 16 marks out of 24.

Overall, this candidate would be awarded a grade A, despite a slightly disappointing answer to part (e).

■ ■ ■

Answer to question 5: candidate B

(a) Source 1 was written by von Papen, and is good for explaining why Hindenburg wanted to support Hitler. Basically it says a civil war would start if they broke the constitution, so because of that they had to choose Hitler. Meaning Hitler was the only man left for the job, and if they did anything else it would have caused a civil war. Hitler was also chosen because he had a big following, and was in with the conservatives like General von Schleicher mentioned in the source. Hindenburg didn't like Hitler because Hitler had stood for the President's election when Hindenburg had also stood. But even because of this he had to be chosen while there was still a constitution. This is why von Papen says Hindenburg agreed to appoint Hitler as Chancellor.

(b) 'Within the framework of the constitution' is an important phrase that could be interpreted in many ways, but is in fact only one thing. It means in the way things are done in the Weimar Republic and probably is used because things that happened in Hitler's rise to power happened within the framework of the constitution. In fact, it can be said clearly that Hitler came to be Chancellor within the framework of the constitution. The constitution was important because it believed in democracy as proportional representation, which was also part of the reason Hitler became Chancellor, which is why the phrase is important.

(c) Source 3 agrees with Source 2 because they are both about the state controlling the rights of individual parties to have opinions for themselves. Source 3 says how the SPD in Northeim could not hold their meetings or pass out their campaigning literature. It also says how they could only have one advertisement in the newspaper and this was done very carefully because they had always been refused before that time. Source 2 is a letter from the British Ambassador in Germany about almost the same sort of thing. It is like Source 3 because it is talking about how they controlled the newspapers, and the entirety of the media, without any complete reason for at least the people who wanted to have their ideas in the newspaper. It explains about the press decrees of 6 February, which gives the government power to suppress a newspaper 'once and for all'. As the source shows, this was difficult for the opponents of the state. So it is easy to see that Source 3 does support the opinions expressed in Source 2.

(d) Source 4 is a table of election results, which are from March in 1933, and shows how successful the Nazi Party were in Northeim. But this does not mean that they were popular because Source 3 also shows that their opponents didn't stand a chance, because they were not able to put their advertisements in the newspaper, which meant that they couldn't attract lots of different people to vote for them. But because the Nazis were in power in 1933 they had power over the town, and so could take out their advertisements, which meant that they could win as they did indeed. It is also obvious that this was true because all the parties that the Nazis hated (like the KPD, the Centre and the SPD) hardly got any votes. But the parties that the Nazis liked (like the DNVP and the DVP) did well or better than the left parties.

(e) The Nazis were very good at consolidating their power, which is obvious from the two sources. It is because of this ability that they became so liked and were successful as a party, although tremendously awful in what they did.

Source 3 is all about the fact that Hitler had power over the people that voted in the elections, and could make it hard for the other parties that wanted to be involved in the elections. Source 3 is particularly about the town of Northeim, where the SPD (the socialists) were forced to become very sly in advertising in the newspaper, because the Nazis were in control of what could be published. But the consolidation of their power was not only because of their power over the media, but also because they were very popular. This was true for a lot of reasons. One of the reasons was that Hitler was a very good speaker who made people feel good when he spoke. Hitler also had a very modern image in comparison with the old people who ran Weimar Germany. More than this, Hitler was good at sensing the hatred of Weimar Germany and the fear of communism, which he played up to. The SS and SA were also important for their consolidation because they forced people to support them.

Another important thing about the consolidation of power was the way Hitler worked his way in the political world of the constitution. Source 5 is good for this because it shows how Hitler manipulated his way to the top. Source 5 explains how Hitler outplayed two of the most powerful of cabinet members in his skill. These two people were von Papen and Hugenberg. The source shows how he managed to convince them that the dissolution of the Reichstag was the right way to go, knowing that this would get rid of them. It also explains how the NSDAP received money from big business, which made Hitler a good candidate for the Chancellor. It is absolutely important to look at the role of Oskar, the son of Hindenburg, who helped Hitler into power. There is also General von Schleicher who couldn't unite the different groups into a coalition.

So there are different things with Hitler's consolidation of power. One of them is the popularity of the Nazis and their control of the media. Another is Hitler's ability to manipulate people into helping him become Chancellor and remove opposition.

e This response is included as an example of a very poor answer. It would be a useful exercise for candidates to go through and analyse what is wrong with each of the responses.

The response to part (a) is poorly expressed. The candidate turns the threat of civil war into a certainty. There is valid appreciation of Hitler's large following, which would earn 2 marks.

The answer to part (b) is repetitious and also badly expressed. It contains a couple of valid points and would gain 4 out of 10 marks.

In the answer to part (c) there is an attempt to link the two sources, but it lacks precision and would gain only 4 marks out of 10.

The response to part (d) does try to assess the value of Source 4 in the light of Source 3, but it fails to pick up on the obvious point that these sources relate to only one small area of Germany which might not be typical of the whole country. This answer would be at level 2: 6 out of 10 marks.

The essay, part (e), lacks real focus on the events of January to March 1933. The useful information in Source 5 to which it refers is not sufficiently amplified with detailed own knowledge. The response is heavily source-based and lacks precise focus in either expression or fact. It would be awarded at level 2: 9 marks out of 24.

Overall, this would be a borderline pass/fail.